# Developing An Appropriate Digital Marketing Strategy Model For Culture In Australia

A Final Thesis Presented to
The Academic Department
Of the School of Business and Economics
In Partial Fulfillment of the Requirements
For the Degree of Doctor in Marketing

## Jarungjit Tiautrakul
ID UD59153BMA68177

# Table of Contents

# List of Tables and Figures

# CHAPTER 1
# General Introduction

## 1.1 THE CONTEXTUAL DATA

Many times digital investment in many organizations usually do not continue after doing for a while. When having the opportunity to talk to many executives, it will find the answer whether it is already done, not seen to be successful like other organizations, do not work effectively, do not happen then until causing many businesses take off the mind or stop doing digital. Doing digital does not start with choosing a platform or develop tools just because seeing their businesses do. The most important role of various technologies is to make the things that we really want to be effected, so the desired results will set the business for the real move forward. Digital work should not be planned year-by-year, but should create a digital roadmap first, which may be defined as the direction of the organization for a period of about 3-5 years because if far more than that, things that are planned may have a new business model that disrupt until not possible in the future (Streich, D., 2014).

There are many technologies for digital marketing, so choosing to use properly need to focus on the technology enabler that will fulfill the business experience that really wants to create for the customer. The choice of technology comes with the appropriate problem set. In an era where Data is the future of business, the investment to create or buy tools must be consistent with the data that they want to obtain and those data that customers must be willing to give to the business willingly, Use of tools need to take into account both users whether ready to use or not, helping their life better, and must take into account that the experience can be transmitted that the business wants to communicate; for example, mobile applications may not be suitable for certain types of businesses because customers may not have the opportunity to buy again. Some businesses are newly set up. Creating a Mobile Application for customers may not have enough motivation to download to use (Benghozi, P., 2015).

For a period of half a century, international business operations focused on marketing that focused to be a key factor in driving the country's economy and society to progress and progress (Kotler & Armstrong, 2014). Especially, there was an innovation of Internet technology in the business called DSMM (Digital, Social Media and Mobile) which affected the progress and growth of the social economy and had a direct impact on consumers and businesses (Lamberton & Stephen, 2016). Especially the interaction between business and consumers, organizational changes and new business opportunities of all sizes (Taiminen & Karjaluoto, 2015) .

Internet technology has been recognized as having a direct impact on business operations and consumer behavior in various countries. Around the world in the last 15 years (Lamberton & Stephen, 2016). "Digital marketing" (Digital marketing) has been frequently mentioned in all aspects of management. Sometimes you may hear the word "Online marketing" (Online marketing) or "Marketing Electronic commerce "(E-Commerce marketing) or" Internet marketing "(Internet marketing). These 3 words had many scholars and experts giving similar meaning that indicated that they could be used inter-changeably (Wymbs, 2014; Chaffey & Ellis-Chadwick, 2016). Digital Marketing refered to the marketing of Internet and electronic media to work together Enabling buyers and sellers to communicate in two ways communication and interact (Interaction) with selected media such as mobile websites, digital TV, IPTV (Internet Protocol Televisions) or other wireless digital media (Chaffey & Ellis-Chadwick, 2016). What is the meaning of this word? Wymbs (2014) explains that the term Digital marketing had a more comprehensive meaning than Internet marketing because digital marketing included communication in all channels of media such as mobile, digital TV, including the internet as well. Buyers and sellers can interact easily causing benefits and values in terms of efficiency, ease, convenience, speed and cost reduction in consumer purchasing decisions including reducing the management costs of the company (Chaffey & Ellis-Chadwick, 2016). Another important benefit of digital marketing is executives can use data from buyers, whether they are B-to-B or B-to-C, to analyze to determine a marketing strategy that will meet the needs of consumers more (Leeflang, Verhoef, Dahlstrom, & Freundt, 2014).

## 1.2 BACKGROUND INFOMATION

Changes in the economic, social, population and development of Internet technology made the marketing process that changed from traditional marketing to more digital marketing (Kotler, Kartajaya & Setiawan, 2017). Both buyers and sellers could be able to interact quickly and easily through the media of choice. As a result, businesses must focus on managing information management from a large number of transactions that called Big data to enable those large amounts of data to be used for business analytics to gain insight into market changes and buying decision behavior of target groups more clearly (Chaffey & Ellis Chadwick, 2016; Taiminen & Karjaluoto, 2015), which would help organizations could plan and formulate marketing strategies that are more suitable for target customers more efficiently and effectively. The digital marketing was quick acception. It could be said that it was because of the integration of various technology systems that called digital convergence which gave to rise technology. That was effective but with a lower cost 3 key technologies: computer technology, communication technology and technology that related to media contents (Kotler, Kartajaya, & Setiawan, 2017). The integration of these 3 technologies created a change in the business and marketing model which increased the value of modern business practices which changed the traditional marketing process into this digital marketing. There were marketing scholars who wrote the book "Marketing 4.0" (Kotler, Kartajaya, & Setiawan, 2017). Interesting observations were 4 things that can be summarized as follows:

1) Market segmentation strategy which previously used various

criteria in the segmentation of markets such as demographic, geography, personality and lifestyle (Psychographic) and behavior. In the future, these criteria will no longer be used in market segmentation, but these criteria will be used together (Kotler, Kartajaya, & Setiawan, 2017). Therefore, many groups of customers who had motivation, demand and different needs, but lived in the same society or market as the customer community, which the author will call "Customer Community" by the community that customers with many subgroups were composed of people of different ages, occupations, status, personality education, and life style, etc. Those people will be able to meet the needs of each group thoroughly, and was able to meet the connected needs. An interesting question for the future of digital digitization is business operators that will be able to use digital marketing to meet customer needs. How many groups that have different motivations and needs, which products / services that will meet that need should be connected, such as education, finance, real estate, take care of your health, tourism, and recreation etc.

2)  Traditional marketing using marketing mix strategy, ie product, price, distribution channel And marketing promotion To blend in to deliver value to the target customers But when the world moves into the digital age, this traditional marketing mix strategy will not be able to respond to complex business operations. The 4Ps strategy will change to The new strategy is called the 4Cs, that is, (1) sharing creativity (Co-creation) (2) Digital currency system (3) Communal activation (4) Negotiation and trading (Conversation and commercialization) Both 4Cs are marketing mix strategies. Connected marketing mix (Kotler, Kartajaya, & Setiawan, 2017). The form of marketing using the 4Cs strategy will see more in the future, whether it is international marketing. Or intergovernmental trading with the government (G-to-G). The question is how to make Marketing in the future that needs to change the marketing strategy from 4Ps to 4Cs can occur most efficiently and effectively.

3) Marketing in the digital age requires customer care to meet the needs of various needs (Kotler, Kartajaya, & Setiawan, 2017). Whether in the same company or in some cases, different companies must collaborate; especially, in the field of data sharing to help agencies or companies get information and can solve problems for customers more accurately and in time by taking into account mutual benefits (Mutual benefits) in delivering the value of products and services to customers such as life insurance businesses that need to coordinate with hospitals, logistics business that requires vehicles to transport goods, both land and air, as well as laws and taxes. The tourism business must coordinate closely with hotels or restaurants in foreign countries to offer the things that meet the needs of the customers as much as possible, etc. The question is how to make the collaboration between agencies more effectively to deliver the value that customers want is the heart of future digital marketing.

4) Digital transformation has resulted in changes in the business model including the occurrence of digital disruption, which means changes caused by digital technology that will create a new business model that will affect the traditional business model (Kotler, Kartajaya, & Setiawan, 2017) such as taxi services: Grab via the top application mobile is a new choice of travel that has been popular today, or hotel business: Airbnb disruption is caused by changes in the competition of the modern business with internet technology being an important factor, so businesses that will survive need to adjust themselves quickly; otherwise, the original business operation will have problems and may be lost. Marketing in the digital age must make customers to have experience better and more impressive. Geraldine Calpin, a former CMO of the Hilton Group, said that modern business operations require modern and accurate information. The emergence of digital disruption or digital transformation cause obstacles for businesses that are not prepared changes in the digital age. Working in this digital age, Calpin calls "Phygital" that means the physical world merges

with the digital world and creates value (Value) for individual customers (Personalization) as much as possible using just an existing Smartphone (CNBC. 2017. Hilton Hotel Chief Marketer: We want to personalize bedrooms using digital technology. [ONLINE] Available at: https://www.cnbc.com [Accessed 17 June 2018]) The question is what to do and how to do about working style to create an impressive experience for customers and increase the work efficiency of employees as much as possible to create a business that has truly different.

As mentioned above, all 4 items are the essence of the transition from traditional marketing to digital marketing. Businesses around the world need to adapt to digital marketing resulting in many questions related to marketing operations including suppliers, wholesalers, retailers, employees and all stakeholders in the process or system of work from production, marketing, sales, management, duties, support various to deliver valuable products or services to customers. Digital marketing research is necessary to help provide information that will help understand the situation and environmental factors both inside and outside of digital marketing, and help formulate a strategy for business planning or marketing that faces future changes; especially, in developing countries with diverse cultures to increase competitiveness.

The current business world is very competitive, Australia is one of the Asia Pacific regions where digital marketing has developed both in marketing and technology that facilitates consumers and is growing rapidly because Australia is home of immigrants from Europe, China, Asia and recently Africa with cultural diversity, became investors interested in selling products in Australia (Thai Trade Centre, 2017). According to Wymbs, 2014, it could show that affected by technology, digital marketing is continually changing. Digital marketing has enabled a two-way-communication, between the marketer and the target audience. This was not possible in traditional marketing, which only offered a one way communication process. Australian culture is rich in diversity. The migration population in Australia is significant, and that has made the country heterogeneous culturally. Although English is widely spoken, there are other languages like Mandarin and

Arabic. More than 330,000 Australians speak mandarin. This makes Australia a reflection of the world culture. Effective marketing strategies need to be conscious of culture (Rao, 2014, p.38). Australia is home of immigrants, from Europe, China, Asia and recently Africa. According to the 2016 census, the total percentage of overseas-born Australian was 33.3% (Abs.gov.au, 2018). Of the 66.7% of the population born in Australia, most are a first and second generation of those borne overseas. Also, the natives, who are Aboriginals, exhibit different culture from what the majority whites do. Chinese, Indians and Philippians formed the largest overseas-born Australians respectively. This indicates how Australia provides a diverse cultural background to marketing firms (Pires, 2015, p. 279).

From the studies about Australian culture, the strategy applied should reflect the culture and way of life of the target audience. Digital marketing techniques have deviated from the traditional marketing techniques in that it seeks to engage the consumer in the marketing process. Digital marketing is experiential, meaning personal values have effects on the way marketer presents products and services to the consumer. Experiential marketing has been shown to have a more significant influence on the target audience. Digital marketing, enabled by a two-way communication. Every consumer has personal and social values that are considered socially and culturally acceptable. The objective of the marketer is to reach more audience and engage them effectively. Efficient marketing utilises the sensory experiences of the target audience and invokes their feelings, reflects on their experiences, their behaviours, lifestyles and relates to their social experiences. Digital marketing capitalizes on modern marketing strategies that seek to use the audience's experience by developing a content that reflects the target customer's social exercise, feelings, sense, behaviours, and cognitive ability. The way people think and act is defined by culture. This means behaviours exhibited by people; to some extent is a reflection of cultural influence (Gabrielsson, M. and Pelkonen, T., 2015).

From the above study about digital marketing techniques and the way people think and act is defined by culture, it may be that culture affects how people think and act. Every culture has different norms that are socially accepted. Any breach exhibited by the marketing team is seen a put-off and creates consumer ethnocentrism and animosity. Willingness to buy a particular product or service that seems not to conform to the personal value of the target audience is affected negatively. Australia, being a culturally diverse country, modern digital techniques applied are affected by the diverse culture. Effective and efficient marketing strategy using digital media should engage the audience in the marketing process. The target audience should be involved in the marketing process, and make the audience feel part of the story. This research is essential to the digital marketer, as it will give direction and strategy that it will be applied in reaching the diverse culture of the Australian market. It will highlight the effects of the diversified culture in the Australian market, and how the multicultural nature of Australians has shaped modern digital techniques.

## 1.3 THE AIM OF RESEARCH

The long-term aim of this research is to understand the relationships between the digital marketing techniques applied by the Australian firms or firms targeting the Australian audience and the culture of the audience. The objective of this study is to provide a comprehensive review of marketing industry practices and literature on the effects of cultures on digital marketing techniques. It will analyze modern digital marketing techniques applied by firms in Australia, technique effectiveness and assess whether these techniques are affected by the diversified culture in the Australian market. Specifically, this research has the following sub-objectives:

1) To study the problems and needs of the digital marketing strategy model that is suitable for culture in Australia.

2) To develop a digital marketing strategy that is suitable for culture in Australia.

3) To evaluate and confirm the appropriate digital marketing strategy model for culture in Australia.

## 1.4 HYPOTHESIS

The digital marketing strategy development affected the cultures in Australia.

## 1.5 CONCEPTUAL FRAMEWORK

The study of the developing an appropriate digital marketing strategy model for culture in Australia, the researcher established the conceptual framework for using in the research as shown in figure 1.1 showing the conceptual framework for using in the research.

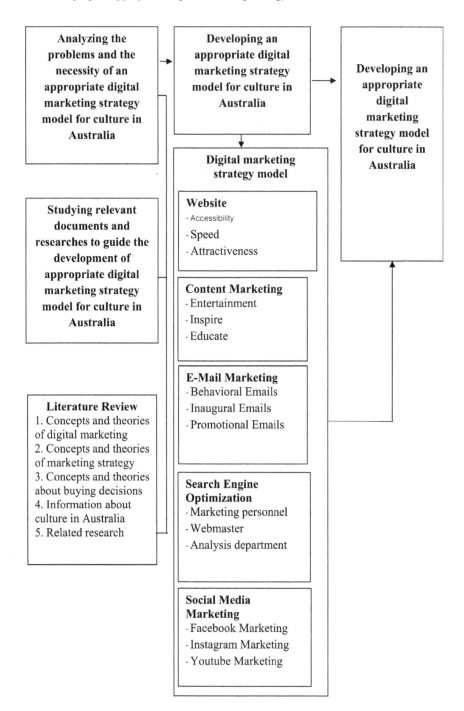

Figure 1 : CONCEPTUAL FRAMEWORK

## 1.6 SCOPE OF THE STUDY

### 1.6.1 Content

This study focused the developing an appropriate digital marketing strategy model for culture in Australia

### 1.6.2 Population and Sample

This study comprised 400 people who were major nationalities and the ethnic background of Australians (18 years and above) in Sydney, Melbourne, Perth, Adelaide, Darwin, Brisbane, and Canberra that data was be collected top six multicultural cities as per 2016 census. Convenient sampling was be sued to find potential respondents that meet specific criteria. Convenient sampling also was known as accidental sampling was defined as a non-random sampling method where members of the population that met a particular criterion like age, accessibility, and willingness to participate.

### 1.6.3 Area

The location used for data collection in this study were Sydney, Melbourne, Perth, Adelaide, Darwin, Brisbane, and Canberra, Australia.

### 1.6.4 Time

Duration of study and research was from 2013 to 2018.

## 1.7 SIGNIFICANCE OF THE STUDY

The result of this research will be valuable to digital marketers and Australian firms in shaping and designing effective digital marketing strategies in a multicultural society like Australia while appreciating the diverse cultural background. Companies targeting Australian multicultural population will know how best to develop and disseminate marketing content that reflects their needs. This will make them engage better with the target audience and build the brand with the customer through experiential marketing.

## 1.8 DEFINITION OF TERMS

The following terms were defined according to how they were used in this study.

1) **Culture in Australia** refers to multicultural population in Sydney, Melbourne, Perth, Adelaide, Darwin, Brisbane, and Canberra.

2) **Digital marketing** refers to the new marketing model developed from traditional marketing by marketing via digital channels to create marketing activities and communication to consumers.

3) **Website** refers to the Host or Server that is registered on the World Wide Web with the service provider on the Internet and able to create their own webpage for trading by consideration of accessibility, speed, and attractiveness.

4) **Content Marketing** refers to marketing in any form with the creation and sharing of content marketing through various forms, especially in online media by consideration of entertainment, inspire, and educate.

5) **E-Mail Marketing** refers to behavioral emails, inaugural emails, and promotional emails by sending brand commercial messages directly to consumers which must have the address of the sender and receiver via the internet system in order to make aware customers, a purchase, and brand loyalty.

6) **Search Engine Optimization** refers to marketing personnel, webmaster, and analysis department for considering the database of web pages that collect search index information, web pages in order to be ranked first to show search results.

7) **Social Media Marketing** refers to Facebook marketing, Instagram marketing, and YouTube marketing that are the medium on the internet which created on the basis of Web 2.0

technology that allows individuals to participate, create and exchange ideas.

8) **Purchase Decision** refers to choosing alternatives with multiple options by considering and compare various elements to get what you want.

9) **E-Commerce** refers to the business activities using electronic media. Through the internet network.

# CHAPTER 2
# Definition of the Investigation

For this study, the review of related literature and studies are presented in the following order.

## 2.1 CONCEPTS AND THEORIES OF DIGITAL MARKETING STRATEGY MODEL

### 2.1.1 Definition of Digital Marketing

This section aims to review the definitions of digital marketing. The following are some of the outstanding definitions.

Allen (2015) state that the use of the Internet, other digital media, and technology to support modern marketing.

Supot Gulati, Montri Verayankura, and Sirawit Sirirak (2017) states that using digital media to market via the internet system to promote the organization, products and services that reach the target group and make decisions in buying and selling products and services that is not complicated, which can be done in several ways:1) social media marketing 2) content marketing 3) website marketing because it has gained a lot of popularity and is mentioned in books, articles and related research.

Summary of the meaning of digital marketing is a new marketing model that is developed from traditional marketing by marketing via digital channels to create marketing activities and communication to consumers.

### 2.1.2 Concepts and Theories of digital marketing

Digital marketing is becoming popular because of the convenience of use, reaching a large number of people and reduce costs rather than other forms of marketing. Digital marketing has 5 important ways to proceed as follows:

- Data management planning can measure the response from the number of visitors to the website, or those who register to participate in the activity enabling marketers to plan and manage existing data systematically to lead to complete data collection process.

- Providing freedom to consumers because many types of Internet users have different needs. If the website is not effective, there is no information that consumers want. Therefore, advertising should be relevant to the content of the website and add creativity to attract the attention of consumers.

- Convenient and fast at present, there are many interesting and interesting websites effect Internet advertising that is outstanding and provides information that meets the needs of consumers that not emphasizing extravagant words that make them unattractive. It also develops advertising strips or banners to be up-to-date and link to the website quickly.

- Check the brand image regularly because people are free to express their opinions. Therefore listening to consumer feedback is another image that the brand should be aware of it. Then bring opinions or problems to improve and develop to create a credible image for the organization.

- Creating diversity in public relations Internet media is another media that can add more interest to the product, such as the introduction of the full movie version, not broadcast on television, to post to the website. To create a stream and create more interest for the brand Moreover, advertising via internet is a cost reduction, and reduce advertising resources that are equivalent or more than event-based advertising (Marketer, 2014: Online).

Natthaphon Phaiphirot (2015) states that the influence of technological advances that include both high-speed internet and devices that access the internet anywhere, anytime effecting digital marketing is important, which means the survival of that business. Digital marketing has a variety of tools for marketers to choose to use marketing strategies. If choosing a variety of tools and appropriate, it will make it more successful.

Aaker (2016) states that digital marketing has four different purposes: offering by adding value to products or services, support for offering and using, expanding other branding platforms by having more dimension and participation, and the last one is center on customers from the interests and activities that customers participate. If not aware of the difference of these objectives, it will result in digital marketing not being effective.

Nares Laopanarai (2017) states that digital marketing is growing rapidly and continuously that can be seen from the advances in strategy, adaptation of brands and companies. Current innovation and new technologies begin to play a role in digital marketing which has 3 trends as follows: 1) The combination of traditional media and online media in the past, television, radio, print media have been reduced in popularity from online media that are constantly growing. Thus allowing the traditional media adjusts the online media to increase advertising effectiveness, such as television programs being broadcast through online media, radio programs can be heard through online media. 2) From software to hardware, online marketing in the past focuses on the use of websites and social media software, but in the future, online marketing will start to use more hardware by using technology (VR) that requires VR glasses to view which create more novelty in digital marketing. 3) In addition to the screen, The success of Pokemon Go shows that modern digital content that no need to depend on the screen. Customers can go out with many brands that have joined the market with this game. Recently, the Alibaba website has produced games on smartphones that have AR technology to find a red envelope as a discount to buy products that is a new market development to attract interest from consumers.

### 2.1.3 Digital Marketing Tools

Tiago, M. T. P. M. B., & Veríssimo, J. M. C. (2014) stated that because the present is the digital age in which technology plays an important role in changing consumer behavior, and is a channel that creates opportunities for business operators, the important key in choosing the right digital marketing tool to attract consumers in the changing era which the commonly known digital marketing tools are as follows:

### 2.1.3.1 Website

It is like a storefront that makes the target group perceive brand reputation, quality, trust and confidence. The website can also be combined with marketing tools which is an additional communication, channel data collection, and create a network of more targeted customers. The first page of the website is intended to invite members and to receive information for being medium for distributing information to inform the promotion and to sell products.

### Definition of the website

Pattharawadee Rienmanee (2014) states that the website is one of the internet marketing media that has played a role in almost all types of business, whether in the form of a company, shop or general business in every parallel of the business because the website can respond and cover consumers or target groups that have no limit because the target group can visit the website information via the internet all over the world 24 hours a day. Therefore, it can be concluded that the website is a storefront that has no scheduled opening and closing and no holidays. Therefore, having a website is very necessary if you want products and services to connect with consumers on the online world.

Wertime and Fenwick (2014) states that the website is currently in an era called Web 2.0, which is very different from the Web 1.0 era. The Web 1.0 era is where the website serves to show information to those who want to watch only, but the Web 2.0 era that is not only used as a data center but the website also serves to distribute to users with more diverse needs, and can modify or browse the information that you need in a short time. There are 4 important and beneficial phenomena for marketers: 1) the separation of presentation and data formats, which makes the proposed data to be reused or presented. 2) new users are involved in creating content, so content is constantly moving, and reflecting the needs of consumers better. 3) there is online community network, and the power of networking is very strong. 4) the use of support technology. With such a phenomenon has led to the inevitable consequences which affects the marketing operations and the marketers are divided into 4 aspects: 1) business competition will be open to everyone equally. 2) the middleman role will be reduce. 3) opportunities of niche markets are endless. 4) the marketing mix is more flexible. Today's websites are different from the past, allowing marketers have to adapt to compete for the advantage of market competition which technology that develops continuously will allow marketers to adjust to accept changes as well.

The website definition is a Host or Server that is registered on the World Wide Web with a rental service provider on the Internet. Then can create their own webpage.

## 8C Framework Website Concept

Structure or working style and the capabilities of the website, researchers and many website developers have developed different website designs to get the proper structure. In this research, the business will focus on electronic commerce websites, which is not only a channel for trading products but also like a storefront. Therefore, the composition of the website is an important factor in the electronic commerce business. It can be divided into 8 areas as follows (Yang, Kim, Dhalwani & Vu, 2014):

1) Website contents are a component of the website content that contains content, the information on the website that is in the form of letters, illustrations, including audio and video files.

2) Context is the structure and design of the website that is the part that makes the website interesting Which is about the color used with the website, images and product presentation form

3) Community is the society in the website of a group of people that consumers can contact, talk or do other activities. It can be shared on the website, such as web boards, chat rooms etc.

4) Communication is a way to communicate with website owners in other ways. This is to increase the convenience of customers such as call center, email, sms, etc.

5) Connection is the ability to link internal and external links

to websites including the ability to search products within websites and external websites as well.

6) Customization is to define the style of the product characteristics to have specific characteristics that are suitable for each customer.

7) Commerce is the process and process of ordering products on the website, allowing customers to make purchases conveniently and systematically

8) Collaboration is to participate in the design and development websites such as feedback and comments, which can be used to improve the website better.

### 2.1.3.2 Content Marketing

Content marketing is an important ingredient for all types of marketing tools, either offline or online. Content must be content and entertainment at the same time. The good content requires creativity, information, knowledge and entertainment. To invite the target group shows some behaviors, such as making a purchase or subscription. Etc. Using the correct vocabulary, the content links products and services seamlessly, not hasty, and uses keywords to help with the dominance of the home page (SEO). Content marketing aims to create brand awareness Create loyalty to the brand Solve the grievances about various issues. Create website traffic to stimulate sales and etc. Marketers have presented the idea of using Internet marketing communications to succeed by focusing on content marketing which is a marketing in the form that offers content at the point, create a distinct, add value and interest. It can make consumers are interested in content resulting in a positive attitude towards the product and motivation in deciding to buy Holliman, G., & Rowley, J. (2014).

## Definition content marketing

Content marketing is a marketing communication approach that focuses on creating interesting content, outstanding with a distinct, identity present various information that is interesting, relevant, able to attract target groups causing the target group to tell word of mouth, and also creating demand for motivation to buy products. In addition, the brand attitude is also increased ("10 differences in marketing ", 2015).

Sheikhahmadi, A. (2014) showed that the important thing in creating content marketing is to create content, which is another marketing strategy for creating and disseminating the importance and value of marketing in order to create attractiveness, acquisition, and association with consumers and to define and understand what drives action that will affect benefits. The purpose of content marketing is to create interest and recognition for consumers by creating content marketing that is always valuable and relevant ("What Is Content Marketing?", N.d.)

Summary of content marketing meaning is to do marketing in any form with the creation and sharing of content marketing through various forms, especially in online media.

## The Importance of Content Marketing

The importance of content marketing is growing that is explained from statistics and the fact that 60% of the B2B business model that entrepreneurs say brands with content marketing helps consumers to make better buying decisions, while 61% of consumers tend to buy products from companies that offer custom content (Gupta, 2014). In addition, 94% of B2B business model marketers use LinkedIn to distribute, 35% define they have a content marketing strategy that is document, while 48% state that they have a content marketing strategy that is not document. In addition, 84% state that the goal of enterprise content marketing is "brand awareness" and 42% of organizations publish new content that supports content marketing every day or several times per week. In general, "content marketing is the art of communicating with customers and your target audience without having to sell. Instead of showing your product or service, back as you send information that makes your buyers smarter. The essence of content strategy is the belief that if we are a business that provides valuable and ongoing information to buyers, they will reward their business and their loyalty in the end. "It is important to know that content marketing is useful in terms of keeping readers' attention and improve brand loyalty. The idea of sharing content to persuade decision makes enabling content marketers to create their own proprietary information content for the selected audience. Alternatively, many content marketers choose to create new information, and share through various media and all media (Gupta, 2014).

The motivation behind content marketing is the belief that providing information to customers effect the brand being recognized as a thought leader and industry expert ("What Is Content Marketing?", N.d.). Explanation "When brands use specific words or stories that resonate with their consumers. They are able to delve into the information that they are consumers by using content marketing, brands can support campaigns and stories about buying patterns and personality (Cohen, 2015).

From the above, that is why it is relevant to your audience and creating an effective brand. You must be trusted and appreciated by creating valuable content and creating interest that changes to a lasting relationship. Content marketing is current and especially in the future of digital marketing and traditional marketing. Therefore, digital marketing strategies cannot be achieved without quality content marketing, and the company needs to conduct thorough research on the target group to create content-oriented marketing that matches the interests of customers.

### 2.1.3.3 E-Mail Marketing

Email marketing, such as news email, promotions, special discounts for customers or members is a way to communicate with the main target group which has the advantage of low cost, fast communication with the target group directly that is a two-way communication that can interact with customers, maintain a good relationship, create impressions, generate traffic and stimulate sales.

### Definition of Electronic Mail

E-mail or Email stands for electronic mail that is a method of exchanging digital messages, which is designed for human's use. The message must contain content, sender's address, and the address of the recipient, which may have at least more than one via the Internet system("Email marketing", 2014). E-Mail Marketing is to send commercial messages to email users or send to current customers. Usually, emails are related to advertisement, sales or donations, and to create loyalty, trust, brand awareness, finding new customers or allowing current customers to make quick purchases ("Email marketing", 2014). E-Mail Marketing is a direct contact between brands and consumers to find new customers or to strengthen brand loyalty. In addition, the brand can also insert an advertisement into the email to encourage customers to purchase products immediately ("Email marketing marketing", 2014).

Summary of the meaning of electronic mail marketing is to send the brand's commercial message to consumers directly, which must have the address of the sender and receiver via the Internet system in order to make customers' awareness, make a purchase and brand loyalty.

### The Concept of Marketing through Electronic Mail

Kantasit Lertpraingam (2014) states that in this electronic age, electronic mail has become an effective communication tool with fast, economical features to reach consumers, and difficult to lose which makes electronic mail a medium that is suitable for direct marketing. In marketing with electronic mail does not only just sending ads to the target group but also marketers can use electronic mail to communicate in many ways. The advantages of electronic mail marketing include direct communication with customers and target groups. Moreover, it's fast and able to respond immediately with low cost, and can communicate with many people at a time. Although the use of electronic mail marketing has advantages, it must also be careful in the delivery of electronic mail in large quantities or without content (Spam). Before using marketing through electronic mails, it must first be accepted by the customers or target group of account owners, and also be able to stop receiving news because it may affect the image of the brand at an irreparable level.

Jackson & DeCormier (2014) states that email is recognized as a communication with marketers to create a relationship that is allowed and real-time interaction with customers.

Wreden (2014) states that email marketing is accuracy in targeting and tracking emails, low cost, and digital processing helps companies to send many emails.

Peppers & Rodgers (2014) claim that clear benefits including the rate of high response and low cost help to make email marketing that is a valuable tool.

Muller (2014) explains that creating an authorized email database can be valuable tools in CRM, offering straightforward alternatives, save the cost of receiving customers and strengthen relationships with customers. In addition, email helps marketers to have more channels to continually reach consumers to create brand identity and consumer loyalty, which email marketing makes consumers more engaged with the brand, and this increased participation shows the intention of buying and positive advice on word of mouth recommendations.

### Types of Email Marketing

Georgieva (n.d.) explains that email marketing can be divided into 6 categories different goals as follows:

1) Email newsletter: business and many organizations send email newsletter to be the first brand they think of the recipient.

2) Digest: subgroups should be easier to use than newsletters because generally consists of lists and links that allows members to scan emails quickly and click the most interested sections by placing the most important call-to-action on top and measuring click-through rates.

3) Dedicated Email: information about a single offer such as notifying the target group about a new document, launching or inviting them to participate in activities that the brand has provided, and help stimulate customer decisions as well.

4) Proactive process of nurturing and managing the relationship with the target customer (Lead Nurturing) is an inbound marketing strategy. Proactive process that involves understanding the different types of sales opportunities, and the need to use email that is connected with consistent objectives and useful content.

5) Sponsorship Emails make access to different groups of people and get new sales opportunities. Sponsored email campaigns are one component of payment strategies. It is important to evaluate and verify reliable partners.

6) Transactional Emails are messages that are stimulated by specific actions that the contact has taken and made them can complete the process.

### 2.1.3.4 Search Engine Optimization

Ranking of websites in the first search engine list for the target group to see the website and receive attention from the target group when you click to watch first access to products and services effect decisions to buy easier.

### Definition of Search Engine Optimization

According to Google's default search engine optimization guide of Google (2014), search engine optimization (SEO) is a set of modifications and techniques, which helps search engines collect index data and understand the content of the website more easily.

Malaga (2008) explains that search engine optimization (SEO) are just a database of web pages, how to find web pages, indexing, and how to search the database. search engine optimization rely on hyperlinked software to search for new web pages, indexing, and updated regularly. Search Engine Optimization (SEO) is to make a website or web page update in order to be ranked first on the search engine with natural methods or free of charge through the target of the desired search term, which is part of marketing via search engine or search engine marketing (SEM).

Summarizing the meaning of search engine optimization is a database of web pages that collect index information, web page search in order to be ranked first to show search results.

## Concepts of Search Engine Optimization

Information or stories without knowledge are often searched on the first page of search engines after checking the search results on the first 5 pages which other pages will not be evaluated by the user. For this reason, moving the page to the top of the search engine is important. In order to achieve this, therefore, requires a website developer to search engine optimization because the page can be moved to the home page of search engines by using only the necessary optimization rules. It is important to have pages that are good looking and efficient structure to introduce the companies, services or products that involve better. It's very important for customers to easily find relevant pages in search engines. In addition, 80% of Internet users are also searching for products or services by using most search engine optimization (Internet3, 2014).

Search engine optimization is a simple and effective way to market for companies that use web pages. In order to achieve this, information that relates to the company will be obtained by using a search engine in a competitive business environment to move up to the top rank. In the search can be done by using search engine optimization. Search engine optimization (SEO) makes the website which appears on the top-rank to display search results for some certain keywords. There are many factors that make the website move up to the top. The most effective way to attract the attention of many users is to connect with search engine optimization because search engine optimization is based on keywords that are appropriate to the website, and can use search with search engines. In order to optimize a website according to search engines, it must be appropriate to the technical conditions (Sezgin, 2014).

Because consumers still choose to receive product information from online, search engine optimization (SEO) becomes increasingly important for integrated marketing communications. SEO planning usually begins with keyword analysis, which appropriate keywords are used and evaluated website content which is created to collect keywords, tags and other text. Moreover, the company has the option to participate in finding paid advertisement, which will be paid to search engines to serve text ads in response to keywords. The success can be measured by analyzing the ranking of websites and visits, impressions, clicks, and references, which these indicators often make it easy to use through the search engine itself (Rutz & Bucklin, 2014).

### 2.1.3.5 Social Media Marketing

Marketing on social media through websites that provide social media services such as Facebook, Twitter, Pinterest, Google+ etc. is a two-way communication that helps to respond to the needs of the target group as well, which social media is a powerful tool and influence with the consumer group very much.

### Definition of Social Media Marketing

Pasin Pitithanarit (2014) states that the meaning that is used very much is caused by 2 concepts, namely Web 2.0 and User Generated Content (UGC). Web 2.0 is a method by software developers and users that take advantage of the Internet, which is the content and various usage patterns are created and published by any one while able to change the form by many users who come from participating at all times. UGC means the user is the creator of the content itself, which has various forms, and publishes in public areas. In summary, social media is a group of various usage patterns on the Internet which can be built on the basis of technology and ideas of Web 2.0, and allow changes to create various forms from the users.

Patchara Kerdsiri (2014) states that social media is a network for creating media that has many social responses by people who create media using the Internet's easy accessibility. In fact, social media arises from the basic needs of humans. In being a social animal that requires interaction and wants to see each other in the first time in Web 2.0 era.

Social media means electronic media which is a medium for the general public to participate in creating and exchanging opinions through the Internet. These media belongs to companies that provide services through their websites, such as Facebook, Twitter, Wikipedia, etc. In technically, social media refers to a group of programs that operate using the basics and technologies of Web 2.0, and in business calls social media as Consumer-Generated Media or CGM for groups of people who communicate with each other through social media. In addition, it may also do activities that are of mutual interest.

In summary, the meaning of social media is the medium that is on the Internet that built on the base of Web 2.0 technology that allows people to participate, create and exchange ideas.

## Concepts of Social Media

Phisek Chainirun (2014) defines social media marketing is a new dimension in marketing that is very different from traditional marketing very much from the same way that marketers communicate with one another, but in an age where we can find information via website, the opportunity for us to believe in the same media is less while believing words from close-minded people who use real or marketing influencer rather than allowing the company to not be able to control the direction of the media. The development of websites that allow people to have the opportunity to develop content on their own cause social media in various forms such as Facebook, Twitter or YouTube that allow people to create content and media to the public causing interaction with others. Social Media Marketing enables customers to update information about new products and services at all times (Weinberg & Pehlivan, 2014). It also helps customers to collect market data with relatively low costs (Gallaugher & Ransbotham, 2014) and can identify new market trends which facilitates the development and market orientation (Becker, Greve & Albers, 2014). It also helps to add real-time news, feedback, comments, complaints and suggestions (Trainor, Andzulis, Rapp & Agnihotri, 2014 ).

Kaur (2016) states that social media marketing is a form of Internet marketing that uses various social networks to create marketing communications and brand social goals. Social media marketing mainly covers activities that relate to social content sharing, videos and pictures for marketing purposes, which is a new trend that is growing rapidly in the form that businesses can easily reach the target customers. It can also be defined as the use of social media channels to promote the company's products.

## The Goal of Using Social Media in Business

Phisek Chainirun (2014) explains about the goals of using social media in business as follows:

In order to increase sales, for example, there is a warning message when there is a special discount sale only on the follower on Twitter, or a product review by a famous blogger and marketing influence. When there is impressed and word of mouth, it generates a lot of purchasing power from those who follow, and it is a channel for customers to have the opportunity to express opinions about products or various services.

1) To increase awareness through social media is to try to allow customers to participate in marketing activities, talk to the brand in a friendly manner and feel like a friend.

2) For public relations, direct communication use as the original media, even if too straightforward, but if we don't tell our story alone or have an interesting story, the selection of certain types of social media for public relations can be very effective.

3) To know the feedback from customers is a useful business that requires attention because of sound reflections from customers, not only hearing two people as before, but also continuing to talk. If the business does not go to get to know and manage properly, it may also affect the brand.

4) To increase the number of people entering social media sites,

it is a tool to push more people into the website. In addition, using social media to connect to the main website also increases the number of links because those who have read articles from various social media will continue to recommend to other people for making it top to show search results.

5) To create thought leadership, this goal is main target for social media users at an individual level. Because social media, especially blog, is quite easy to use, it's different from the original website. It makes those who have various expertise having space to express opinions, having written content to educate, and there are many people to follow reading. it makes them a thought leader, and has marketing influence.

### 2.1.4 The Difference between Traditional Marketing and Digital Marketing

Schwenke (2014) describes 10 differences between traditional marketing and digital marketing as follows:

Pattern: They are different. Communication of traditional marketing emphasize clarity, but digital marketing emphasize the most spread without emphasizing the structure.

1) Communication methods: Traditional marketing is 1 to many listeners who will listen only, but digital marketing is many to many that can be sent together.

2) Duration: Traditional marketing uses long-term , but digital marketing is a rough plan, and use fast interaction.

3) Communication with consumers: Most traditional forms are concealed. Using communication via email or phone, but the digital part emphasizes the speed of the public response immediately.

4) Time period: Traditional marketing focus on working hours with ending work, but digital marketing rather free to use to easily reach the consumer group.

5) Scope: Traditional marketing has a specific group, but can be

made as a mass. If it is digital, which is also a mass, it can approach new prospects.

6) The value of the experience: Digital marketing is better and clearer than traditional marketing because they can interact with users, but traditional marketing is analogue.

7) Supervision: Traditional marketing care by protecting consumers and competitors, which digital marketing has the same traditional marketing care but adds users and platforms.

8) Language: Traditional use is formal. But digitally rather free to use in order to easily reach people

9) Care agencies: Traditional marketing has been digitally changed, or having a new department to set up specifically for digital management

From the above ideas, the researcher concludes that the concept of digital marketing tools is a measurement tool for "Digital Marketing" which includes the components of the 8C Framework website of Yang, Kim, Dhalwani & Vu (2014), the importance of content marketing in Gupta (2014), the concept of Georgieva's email marketing type (nd), the concept of search engine optimization the first page of Rutz & Bucklin (2014) and the concept of the social media business use of Phisek Chainirand (2014). The researcher chooses them to use as guidelines in this study because digital marketing effects technology plays an important role to consumers' behavior, and is an opportunity for business operators. The key lies in choosing the right digital marketing tool to attract consumers in the changing era which digital marketing tools that researchers choose are generally known.

## 2.2 CONCEPTS AND THEORIES OF MARKETING STRATEGY

### 2.2.1 Definition of Marketing

Academicians have given different meanings of the market, such as the market where is the meeting places of buyers and sellers. The needs of the buyer for a particular type of product and service that is widely distributed both inside and outside the country means that the person or organization with the needs that has wants and the power to buy the product (Lamb, Hair, Mc Danmiel, 2014, p.212, cited in Wanthanee Sanphakdee, 2014).

From above definition, it may be concluded that the market refers to a group of people that must have 3 elements, consisting of a group of people who want the need, have the power to buy, and are satisfied or willing to buy the product. However, in the sale of products, there is no product to market that will be bought all quickly because each customer group is different in lifestyle and environment. Therefore, in the sale of products, the manufacturer must determine the target market that is the group of buyers of products that the company has decided to choose to target customers which can be divided into 5 types as follows. 1) resource markets is the starting point for considering the structure of the modern market when manufacturers operate to procure raw materials, funds for using in the production of products and services such as farmers raising frogs for delivery to groups or communities. Farmers must provide financing to find a place to raise frogs, provide tadpoles and labor to help feed frogs etc. 2) resource markets or business markets are markets that buy products for internal operations or buy for production as finished products such as agriculture in the frog raising community, then send to sell with groups or communities that transforms fresh frogs into canned frogs for further distribution. 3) consumer markets are a market consisting of a number of buyers who purchase products to treat their own needs or household, such as buying rice, toothbrushes, toothpaste, clothing, medicines, etc. 4) intermediary markets is a market that buys products for resale or renting with the objective of seeking profit including middlemen, wholesalers, retailers, brokers, etc. 5) government markets is a market that purchases products for using in operations within government agencies or public services.

Kotler (2014) states that the market as human activities that carry out in order to meet various needs and to create satisfaction by using the exchange process and the activities that are held must satisfy consumers' satisfaction.

Moreover, he defines the market as buying, selling, researching, marketing, advertising warehouses, which is the process of bringing products from the factory to consumers by creating satisfaction for consumers, marketing that means a group of customers who expect that there is a need, willingness and ability to exchange which businesses choose to use business efforts that will bring satisfaction to both consumers and businesses.

From the above marketing meaning, there are issues to consider: marketing must be exchanged. There must be buyers and sellers. Before the trading activity occurs, there must be other marketing activities to help, such as planning activities, pricing, promotion and distribution of products, offering products, services and offering valuable ideas to the target market to meet consumer satisfaction and achieve the objectives of the business organization.

Summary of the meaning of marketing means the planning process, management of product and service concept, price, marketing promotion And distributing products and services As well as ideas for the exchange which brings satisfaction to customers and achieve the objectives of the business organization. Marketing management is the planning process for product, management, concept, product, pricing, distribution. Then marketing promotion for products and services that create exchanges and satisfy customers At the same time, the organization achieves the desired goals

### 2.2.2 Concepts and Theories of Marketing

Suchada Aungsujinda (2015) defines in business, marketing is a must for entrepreneurs to know for allowing buyers and sellers to respond properly and appropriately, and must consider the benefits of the company, customers and society. Whenever there is a conflict of interest, marketers also need to consider priorities for such institutions. Therefore, need to understand the concepts and marketing philosophy to be applied to the business, marketing and philosophy concepts can be divided as follows:

1) The production concept is a concept that emphasizes the ability to produce products or services of the business rather than taking into account the needs. The desire of the buyers of this concept arose in the beginning of the use of machines to produce products, and when there is progress in product manufacturing technology, manufacturers are determined to produce the best products, save the most cost, and believe that if the products and services are of good quality, it will help convince buyers to buy products or services for sure.

2) The product concept is a marketing concept that adheres to consumers' needs for high quality products and can be used well, emphasizing new innovative products Therefore, the seller must offer quality products and must update the product at all times.

3) The selling concept is a concept that focuses on pushing products from manufacturers to the buyers quickly, and as many as possible. For this method, the seller will offer the product and then persuade the customer by using various sales tools, including using sales staff., promotion market until advertising use to encourage the buyer to buy as much as possible. This concept has a weakness that sellers want to sell products or services primarily, and use too aggressive sales concepts by lacking analysis of the real needs of the market. If customers do not have real needs, it will effect in no purchase, may cause the marketing system to be interrupted.

4) The marketing concept is a marketing concept that a business organization can achieve by offering products or services, and effectively communicate value to the target market that is superior to the competition, or is a business that focuses on the

needs and satisfaction of customers and social responsibility in order for the business to exist. In this concept, there are often slogans or warnings such as "The customer is the king" "The customer is always right." "The customer is our master." "The customer is the partner for profit.". L.LB. (L.L. Bean Company), which operates the clothing distribution business and tools for outdoor sports by mail. The company has written posters as a message that motivates their employees to provide services to customers as well, with the following words: "What are customers? Customers are the most important person in this company ... whether in person or by mail. Customers do not rely on us, but we rely on customers. Customers are not interrupting our work ... but customers are our work objectives. Providing services to customers is not to do what is obligation, but the customers that have obligation for us because giving us the opportunity to serve them. The customer is not the person who will fight with, brainwashing or wit ... and no one ever argued the customers and won them. The customer is the person who brings us what he wants ... and that's our job to take good care of them and ourselves. "

5) The social marketing concept is a concept that a business organization considers needs and the satisfaction of the target market that offer products or services that target customers want with superior performance over competitors. At the same time, it can preserve and promote the well-being of society as well. At present, Top businesses organizations have 2 social marketing concepts as follows:

(1) Social marketing that focuses on ethics by focusing on ethics, rules or regulations to occur with society as a whole as well as being generous to help each other including promoting family institutions, religious institutions and others

(2) Social marketing that focuses on the environmental marketing is a product offering to the market by destroying

the environment or creatures of animals, wildlife or the resources of the world to a minimum.

6) Modern marketing concept will see that large modern businesses will try to connect themselves with customers in various ways such as using the latest modern technology to produce and use the service both in the country and outside the country, studying the real needs of customers to obtain information that will improve products and services. There is an expression of social responsibility to create a sense of unity with both the current customers and the general public who are not current customers because of the high competition Therefore, reputable businesses such as Nike, Coke, McDonald's must operate the market with maximum efficiency, and still have to adjust to the market conditions and competitors that change constantly, such as in the past, makes the tailor shop popular while the shirts sold at the store are not popular. Later, the men's shirt brand is popular, and people turned to buy ready-made clothes, making the tailor shop business unpopular. In the early days, the brand of Aero was only popular in one brand before the Sfair GQ and others followed, now became a foreign brand to play a role, so famous brand shirts have more competitors and a strong competitor. If businesses do not develop themselves, their business will not be possible in the end.

### 2.2.3 The Importance of Marketing

Marketing work is a job that involves searching and creating demand for buying including the demand for purchase or demand (Sophin Piyachat, 2018), all types of business organizations need to use marketing as a tool to generate income for the business which will lead to profit making for the business Thai economic system requires marketing to develop social economy, and international trade, especially in today's highly competitive international trade. Marketing is therefore important as follows (Waranya Thikom, 2014).

1) Marketing is important to the economy and society as follows.

(1) Marketing helps generate revenue for the country because marketing helps create demand for products and services This requirement may be an internal and external requirement.

(2) Marketing helps raise the living standards of people because marketing helps stimulate people to think of new products to meet the needs of the people.

(3) Marketing helps to support international trade, and making the market more spacious, so the country can send products to sell.

(4) Marketing helps to create turnover of production factors by using existing production factors to produce products for service to consumers.

(5) Marketing helps increase production in order to increase demand for purchase. Marketing makes more investment and employment, so people don't be unemployed, earn more and have more purchasing power.

2) The importance of marketing to the organization

Marketing is important to the organization as follows:

(1) Marketing is an activity that generates income for the organization and lead to profit generation.

(2) Marketing is creating value for the product causing the business to earn more.

(3) Marketing helps to reduce the cost per unit of production due to the use of marketing tools to increase production volume by using distribution and marketing promotion methods that make the organization able to save money.

(4) Marketing helps business people to have initiative and develop new things to o meet the needs of consumers, and make the business organization growth.

3) The importance of marketing to individuals

Marketing is important to people as follows:

(1) Marketing allows individuals, buyers and sellers to contact, buy and sell products without having to waste time traveling, seeking buyers and sellers.

(2) Marketing allows the seller to produce products that match the needs of the buyer.

(3) Marketing helps buyers or consumers to eat better. When there is a market, there are products that consumers can choose from as many products as they want.

(4) Marketing is creating a career for people because marketing creates a career in production, sales, advertising, etc.

(5) Marketing helps people bring knowledge about marketing to life by applying marketing principles to apply in various occupations

### 2.2.4 Marketing Mix

Marketing mix factors that marketing executives offer to the target market for the treatment of needs as well as bringing the highest satisfaction to the target market (Chattida Kusayanayon, 2014). The marketing mix is divided into 4 elements: product, price, place, and promotion. All marketers call this 4P's marketing decisions that may normally be classified into 4 strategies: 4 P's that are intended for Lahore to combine elements of both strategies is the only 4 to objective that is to combine all 4 strategic elements into harmony. So that the target market that the company chooses can better meet the needs of the competition and is in the direction of achieving the objectives of the company, regardless of profit, or it is not aimed at profits (Phetchara Budsritha, 2012)

### (1) Products

Product means items or services, concepts or practices that is presented to the target market to meet the needs. The desire of the target market to be satisfied by the tangible things that are the identity of things or products. And tangible things that are services, concepts and practices, examples of products include crops agriculture, food, toothpaste, medicine, powder, clothing, shoes, bags, cars, houses, etc. Private services such as medical treatment, masseuse, doctor, city of the north, barber service, sewing service clothes, and beauty services, etc., such as the concept and practice of advertising agency services product introduction services, etc. In determining the marketing mix strategy must also consider who the target customer is. Is a direct consumer Or the mediator who has to sell the product So marketers will determine according to the marketing mix strategy according to the needs of buyers in the target market as Robert Lorraine has proposed the relationship of 4 P's that the activity applies to 4 C's that is related to the customer as follows (Lauterborn, Robert, quoted in Kotler, 2014, p.16).

From the above details offering products to meet the needs of customers or it can be said that the product is the answer to the customer, where the business determines the exchange price for the product, the money that the customer has to pay while the business operates the distribution and distribution of products to places where customers are convenient to find products or products which relies on marketing promotion to communicate and understand, provide information to customers However, when considering both the business and the customer, all 4 above factors will help the client's business to meet the needs of both groups. The products that are tangible can have the following elements:

1) Product variety: the product must have a variety so that consumers can procure according to interest and consumer needs.

2) Quality: products can be produced because the manufacturer has the intention to produce the best. At the same time, the most quality products will have a high price as well. Therefore, the production of products of any quality depends on the needs of the market, and consumers are willing to buy at a price that can be purchased, such as agricultural products, will be divided into grade A, grade B and grade C. Products that are grade A will be priced higher than grade C.

3) Design: design is an important component of the product

because the consumer needs to buy products will depend on two factors. First, the value in the benefits to be used and the spiritual value. Design must focus on the needs of consumers, and customer preferences.

4) Feature: the product must have a distinctive appearance that is unique to the product that customers know and remember.

5) Brandname: it is the name of the product which represents the reputation characteristics, product quality and product confidence.

6) Packaging: shape and appearance of the packaging will be a factor indicating the quality, properties of each product type. They effect in consumer satisfaction.

7) Size: it is an important component of another product. How to make the product size according to the needs of consumers, and must consider how many sizes should be each size should have a pattern.

8) Service: some products need to be serviced together with the use of the product, such as refrigeration and washing machine, etc. need to have service check for free after consumers have bought in less than 1 year. Such services will make consumers satisfied, and loyalty in the product

9) Warranties: they are a commitment that if the product purchased by the consumer is damaged in the specified period, the seller will be responsible for the insurance contract.

10) Return: it is an agreement between the consumer and the seller that if the product is not of quality, the seller will return within the agreed period.

Special characteristics of products that do not exist as follows:

1) Intangibility: service sales are different from selling products because the service cannot be seen, tested, heard or sniffed before using the service. Only the service users inquire from the users,

inquire from those who have used the service whether there is quality or not, such as restaurants, hotels, hospitals, beauty salons, traditional medicine services such as foot massage etc.

2) Inseparability: the use of the service will be used immediately and cannot be stored for further use such as Watching movies, car wash services

3) Variability: service is highly variable depending on the service provider. Time and place such as The doctors who treat the sick will find that each patient will have different variances. Therefore, the service provider must be a good service provider to impress the users.

4) Perishability: the service cannot be preserved if not used, such as car wash service, foot massage. If no one comes to use the service during that time, time will run out that cannot be preserved.

## (2) Price

The price refers to the amount of money used to exchange for the purchase of goods or services, whereby the buyer and the seller agree that the price is one part of the marketing plan that will bring satisfaction to the consumer with infection. Value and cause accumulation (utility) suitable for the price or amount paid.

Value means the prioritization of assessments in the form that can create satisfaction for the appraiser is the customer.

Utility means the benefits derived from products that will lead to production of things that are beneficial to consumers in determining product prices. Must be flexible in order to adjust the price to the changing market situation as follows:

Item price means the price that is the reference base in calculating the actual sale price.

Net price means the actual selling price, which may include shipping or not. Normally, it is determined from the discount that the company gives the announcement price.

Product pricing is the most important aspect of marketing because the price plays an important role in the survival of the business. Therefore, it should study the purpose of pricing, pricing procedures, pricing, pricing policies and price strategies

Objectives determination of pricing objectives as a guideline for pricing policies, pricing strategies and pricing methods. So that the company can consider various factors that affect the business. The pricing objectives are as follows:

1) Profit maximization: one of the objectives of the business is to have a profit. Therefore, what kind of products are profitable to do business? In determining the most profitable objectives, the financial liquidity or return on investment must be considered and there is a need to know the relationship between demand and cost at various price levels to choose the price that gives the highest return.

2) Rate of return on investment: the determination of this objective because the company must determine the price to get a return on investment that is invested in production, such as machinery, tools in the factory, product research and development and other expenses, including business efforts.

3) Revenue maximization: the objective is to set the appropriate price for the business that cannot clearly identify the production cost, such as the business that gives the employee compensation in the form of a commission from the sale in calculation.

4) Market share maximization: the price is expected to be long-term by occupying the same market and expanding the market to expand to create opportunities for the business to be a market leader. This objective is suitable for businesses that have a product cycle in the growth stage.

5) Maintain share: pricing is based on the market level so that the business will continue to be a leader in the market.

6) Maximization of customer volume is the objective of the

business that has a high cost. When customers increase, the cost will be reduced and this objective is suitable for profit-seeking businesses.

7) Minimization of customer volume: it is an objective setting that is suitable for businesses that have outstanding, special characteristics, and value in the eyes of consumers who are specific customers. Pricing determines the high price to limit the number of customers, such as members of the famous golf course.

8) Meeting competition: pricing will use the price level that is in the market in order to avoid price competition in the market, but the business must compete by using other marketing mix to help, such as creating differences in products, distribution and marketing promotion etc.

9) Product quality leadership, an objective for businesses that have very good quality products. Pricing is high, so this high price reflects the excellence of the product.

10) Skimming maximization: it is the objective that is suitable for businesses that introduce new products to the market. Pricing will be high due to the introduction of products. When the sales reach the full growth stage, then gradually reduce the price in order to penetrate other segments of the market

11) Social: it is the price that the company wants to create a public image by setting a lower price that should be a fair price. Including products and services for the public.

12) Survival is the setting of pricing objectives for businesses that are experiencing economic crisis. Causing the purchasing power to decrease, businesses or businesses need to reduce the price of the product to allow buyers enough to buy power in an economic downturn.

For pricing procedure, price is a marketing mix that makes money for the business. Therefore, proper pricing will be important to the profits that arise. And create satisfaction for customers as well. Pricing is as follows.

### (3) Place or distribution

Distribution refers to the structure of channels which consist of institutions and activities. Used to move products and services from the organization to the institutional market that brings products to the target market that is a marketing institution. For the activities that help distribute products, they include transportation, warehousing, and keeping inventory. Distribution consists of 2 parts as follows:

1) The channel of distribution means the path that the product and (or) ownership that the product has changed to the market. In the distribution channel system, it consists of manufacturers, intermediaries, consumers or industrial users.

2) Market logistics means activities related to the movement of products from manufacturers to consumers, or users in the distribution industry, therefore consisting of (1) transportation (transportation) (2) storage and warehousing (warehousing) (3) inventory management.

### (4) Promotion

Marketing promotion is a communication about the information between the seller and the buyer to create an attitude and buying behavior. Communication may use personnel selling to sell and non-personal selling. There are many communication tools that may be used by one or more tools: Integrated marketing communication (IMC) by considering the suitability for customers and competitive products by achieving common goals, important promotion tools are as follows:

1) Advertising is an activity to present news about the organization and (or) service products, or ideas that need to be paid by the sponsor of the program Advertising strategies are related to (1) creative strategy and advertising tactics (2) media strategy

2) Personal selling is an activity to inform and motivate the market using people that will relate to (1) personal selling strategy (2) sales force management.

3) Sales promotion means promotion activities other than advertising, personal selling and providing news and public relations which can stimulate interest, trial or purchase by the final client or other person in the sales promotion channel. There are 3 types of sales promotion: (1) consumer promotion (2) trade promotion (3) sales force promotion.

4) Publicity and public relation: giving news is an idea about products or services that do not require payment. The public relations means efforts that are planned by one organization to create a positive attitude towards the organization to one group. Giving news is an activity of public relations.

5) Direct marketing or direct response marketing, and online marketing is a communication with the target group to respond directly or refer to various methods. That marketers use to promote products directly to buyers and cause immediate responses, including (1) telephone sales (2) sales using direct mail (3) sales using catalogs (4) Sales on television, radio or newspapers that motivate customers to have response activities such as using coupons to buy.

In addition, Kotler (2000) is considered a concept that is related to the business that provides the service, which will receive marketing mix (7Ps) in determining the marketing strategy as follows:

1) Product is the thing that satisfies the needs and needs of human beings. What the seller must give to the customer and the customer will receive the benefits and value of that product. The product is divided into 2 types: products that may be tangible and intangible products.

2) Price means product value in the form of money Customers will compare between the value of the service and the price of that service. If the value is higher than the price, the customer

will decide to buy. Therefore, pricing of services should be appropriate to the level of service clearly, and easy to classify different service levels.

3) The distribution channel (Place) is an activity related to the environment in offering services to customers which affects the perception of customers in the value and benefits of the services offered which must be considered in terms of the location and the channels for offering services.

4) Promotion is one of the tools that are important in communicating to users. With the objective of informing or inducing attitudes and behaviors The use of services and is the key to the relationship marketing.

5) People or employees, which require selection, training, and motivation in order to create satisfaction for customers differently than competitors The relationship between service officers and users of various services of the organization. Service officers must be competent, attitude that can respond to users, initiative, ability to solve problems, and can create values for the organization.

6) Physical evidence and presentation is the creation and presentation of physical characteristics for customers by trying to create overall quality both physical thread and service model to create value for customers whether the dress is clean, neat negotiations must be gentle, and fast service, or other benefits that customers should receive.

7) Process is an activity related to procedures and work practices in the service that offer to users in order to provide accurate and fast service, and make the users impressed.

In summary, the important marketing mix consists of 7 factors as follows: (1) Product is the product model and types of materials that used for production and distribution in the chicken farming equipment business in closed systems farms Including usage (2) Price is to determine which price will be set the price that is consistent with the market or competitors, or the product position of the product (3) Place must be coordinated with the overall marketing plan, and prescribing specific marketing promotion plans (4) Promotion, namely public relations, radio advertising, newspapers, brochures, cloth labels and various activities (5) People are employees which require selection, training, motivation to be able to create satisfaction for customers differently than competitors. Is the relationship between service providers and users of various service organizations. The service provider must have the ability, attitude that can respond to users with originality, the ability to solve problems, and can create values for the organization (6) Physical evidence and presentation is to create and present physical characteristics for customers by trying to create overall quality both physical and service forms to create value for customers whether the dress is clean, neat negotiations must be gentle, and fast service, or other benefits that the customer should receive, and (7) Process is an activity that is related to procedures and work practices in the service that offer to users in order to provide accurate and fast service, and make the users impressed.

## 2.2.5 Marketing Management

Marketing management refers to the planning of operations and control of marketing programs that will bring satisfaction from exchanges with the target market. In order to achieve the objectives of the company, which focuses heavily on the needs of the target market And must be satisfied too By determining the price, selection and distribution effectively in order to inform and stimulate the needs of that market (Supansana Thanayakul, 2014)

Marketing mix factors are very important factors for marketing executives. And is a related factor, that is to say that the market will have to have products or services that will be presented to consumers first. When there is, there must be a price that consumers have to pay or find anything else that has the value as determined. The price will have to produce a difference with the cost of generating profits in order to circulate marketing operations, and must have a place of sales to the consumer and finally, encouraging consumers to be interested in the products and services of the company until promotion is necessary Otherwise it may not be able to sell products.

### 2.2.6 Marketing strategy

The form of marketing strategy can be divided according to the 4 type of product type, namely, convenience products, product selection, Purchased specific products, and unsought goods (Pongsan Tanyong et al, 2014) as follows:

### (1) Convenience products

1) product strategy

1.1) There are many products to choose from (product flanking), regardless of size. color, odor, quality, price to meet the needs of different consumers.

1.2) Multi brand strategy to better reach different target market segments, such as Imperial Company, using multi brand strategy to distribute cookie products, namely Imperial, Violet, Rosiesweettime

1.3) Brand-extension strategy is the use of the original brand that is already popular for the expansion of new products, such as the extension of the Timothy shampoo brand is Timothe hair conditioner, and Timothe shower Gel

1.4) Quality strategy: The company will offer many quality products to choose from.

1.5) Product innovation: The company will try to create new products into the market such as Henna, herbal shampoo that make black hair, Carefree sanitary pads.

2) Price strategy: Price for convenience products that is relatively low in order to sell large quantities, and the flexibility characteristics of demand for the price of this product are high that is a product with a high turnover rate. Products can be used interchangeably, and have many competitors. However, we can

set the price to be different from the market price by making product differentiation.

3) Distribution strategy is a product offering to the target market for convenience products that will be separated into 2 cases:

   3.1) The number of levels of distribution is likely to pass through many intermediaries in order to distribute products to consumers thoroughly, such as from manufacturers through wholesalers and retailers to consumers.

   3.2) The number of retailers that sell convenience products which often use intensive distribution methods because consumers are scattered in general, and the nature of buying products like this, consumers will use less effort to buy.

4) Promotion strategy: convenience products will use the tools to promote the market from the least to the following:

   4.1) Advertising: convenience products must have a lot of advertising to create awareness and product satisfaction for consumers.

   4.2) Sales promotion is a tool that encourages buying decisions with incentives for consumers such as price reduction, gift giving, sweepstakes which are often used to promote advertising to attract consumers to buy more products. This method of advertising and promotion aimed at consumers is called the pull strategy.

   4.3) Sales force is the use of sales staff to contact the store in product placement, and sales promotion at the point of sale to increase sales space, and how to sell effectively.

## (2) Shopping goods

Product selection (This is a product that buyers tend to compare before making a purchase.) Factors for using in comparison including suitability, quality, price and style etc. Examples of this type of products include furniture, clothing, electronics accessories. Product selection are divided into 2 groups as follows:

1) Homogeneous shopping goods means products that consumers see as buying. There are general basic characteristics as well. Therefore, the purchase decision will depend on the lowest price of the product, mainly such as refrigerator, television, student shoes, etc.

2) Heterogeneous shopping goods means the product that the buyer sees that have different characteristics. Therefore must compare aspects of quality, suitability and characteristics more important than price, such as clothes, bags, furniture, etc.

   Marketing strategy for product selection

   2.1) Product strategy: it will be different in terms of style, quality and price so that customers can compare as needed.

   2.2) Price strategy: if it is the same product to buy, price setting is low because the customer holds the price as an important factor in buying, but if it is a different product to buy, the price will be higher or lower depending on the quality, product style and target customer characteristics.

3) Distribution strategy: it will consider the characteristics as follows:

   3.1) The level of distribution tends to be relatively short because of obsolete products. In general, products from manufacturers will pass through retailers to consumers, or use channels from manufacturers through distributors Retailers to consumers In the event that the manufacturer is not convenient to distribute.

   3.2) Selective distribution: it use magazine-type advertising media that corresponds to the target group. Sales promotion focuses on the display of products at the point of sale, where the salesperson must be able to provide details about the product, and have the ability to convince customers.

## (3) Specialty goods

Specific products is a unique product that the customer wants and is willing to use the effort to acquire that product. Moreover, the customers are honest with the brand, so the purchase decision depends on the reputation, quality and pride that can be gained from using the product more than the price, such as shoes (Natureriser), hotel (Oriental hotels), camera (Nikon), perfume (Joy) etc.

Marketing strategies for specific products are as follows.

1) Product strategy must be of outstanding quality, different from the product with its own identity, development, maintained products with outstanding quality, and exotic all the time.

2) Price strategy tends to be higher than normal to show the image of the product. Customers have a small amount and have high purchasing power. There is a need to buy products directly, so holding the benefits to set the price as high as needed or more according to the number of buyers.

3) Distribution strategy will consider 2 cases:

   3.1) The level of distribution is relatively short or the manufacturer sells directly to control marketing policies and maintain the image of the product.

   3.2) The exclusive distribution means the dealer is used, or only one or two retailers in one territory because consumers are loyal to the brand By using high effort to buy products already, so no need to use many retailers.

4) promotion strategy: advertising will focus on brand identity. It often use the media in a magazine that corresponds to the target customer. Sales promotion will focus on product display. Giving free gifts rather than discounting as for sales using salespeople, sales staff must have products and customers, and have a good art of sales as well as having a good personality.

## (4) Unsought goods

Unsought goods is a product that consumers know, but do not think to buy or do not need to buy that be often new products such as food blender, smoke filter, or an old product that consumers know, but do not see the need to use that product such as life insurance, encyclopedia etc. Marketing strategies for unsought goods are as follows.

4.1) Product strategy: product development to meet consumer needs

4.2) Price strategy: the price setting will add a high profit per unit because it is difficult to sell with low turnover.

4.3) Distribution strategy: the number of levels of channels is short, which is often used to direct sales because it is a product that requires sales staff to stimulate demand.

4.4) Promotion strategy: promotion will be in the form of sales using employees, and advertising for consumers to know the product.

## 2.3 CONCEPTS AND THEORIES ABOUT BUYING DECISIONS

### 2.3.1 Definition of Purchasing Decisions

Schifman (2014) defines the meaning of buying decisions as the actions of consumers to make decisions in the form of product selection, brand selection, discount and order's amount for the measurement of purchasing decisions by considering the 3 elements: thinking, interest and the behavior of buying decision.

Kotler (2014) defines the meaning of buying decisions, namely motivation, awareness, learning, personality and attitude that will demonstrate the need, and realize that there are many products to choose from activities that are relevant to consumers in relation to existing information, or the information that is provided by the manufacturer, and the evaluation of those choices are the final.

Chattayaporn Ruengjai (2017) has given the meaning of buying decisions as a process of choosing to do one of the various alternatives that consumers often have to decide on various options of products and services, which they will choose products or services according to the information and limitations of the situation. The decision is an important process and within the minds of consumers.

In summary, the meaning of buying decisions is the process of choosing multiple alternatives by considering and comparing various elements to get what you want.

### 2.3.2 The Concepts of buying Decisions

Kotler (2014) explains that the consumer decision-making process (Decision Process), even though consumers are different, there are different needs, but consumers will have similar buying decisions. The purchasing decision process is divided into 5 steps as follows:

### 1) Need Recognition

The problem arises when a person feels the difference between the ideal condition that the person feels good for himself, and it is a condition that is desirable with the real condition of things that happen to himself, thus causing the need to fill the difference between the ideal state and the reality. The problems of each person will have different causes, which can be concluded that consumer problems may arise from the following reasons:

- The original used items are gone. When the original used items to solve the problem begin to run out, resulting in a new demand from the existing missing items. Consumers need to find new things to replace.

- The result of solving problems in the past leads to new problems. Caused by the use of a product in the past may cause problems such as when a car belt is broken but cannot find the original belt, therefore the need uses other replacement belts that are not standard causing the car to make a loud noise, so had to find a spray to inject the belt to reduce friction.

- Personal change, individual growth both maturity and qualifications or even negative change such as illness, including
physical changes, growth or even the mental state causes new
changes and needs.

- Change in family conditions such as marriage and having
children make to occur a need for products or services.

- Change of financial status whether it is a change of financial
status either positive or negative inevitably effect in a change
of lifestyle.

- The result of changing the reference group: people will have
reference groups in each age, each period life, and each different
social group. Therefore, the reference group is an influence on
consumer behavior and decision making. The effectiveness
of marketing promotion: when promoting various markets
whether it's advertising, public relations, discount, barter,
giveaway, sales by using employees or effective direct marketing
will be able to encourage consumers to be aware of problems
and needs.

In conclusion, when consumers are aware of the problem, they
may or may not find a solution to that problem if the problem is not
very important. It means to fix or not, but if the problem has not disap-
peared, not reduced or increased , the problem will become a stress that
becomes a driving force to try to solve the problem in which they will
begin to find solutions to problems by searching for information first.

## 2) Information Search

When problems occur, consumers must seek solutions by finding
additional information to help make decisions from the following
sources:

- Personal Search is a person as information source such as
family, friends, reference groups, experts or people who have
used that product.

- Commercial Search are sources of information that can

be obtained at the point of sale, company or shop that is a manufacturer or distributor or from sales staff.

- Public Search are sources of news from various media such as television, radio, including searching information from the Internet.

- Experimental Search is the source news that receives from the experience, check, and trial.

In conclusion, some consumers use the effort to search for information to make a purchase decision, but some consumers are less to do it. This may depend on the amount of information that they have in the past, the severity of desire, or the convenience of finding.

## 3) Evaluation of Alternatives

When consumers get the information from step 2, then they will evaluate the options and decide the best way. The methods that consumers use to evaluate alternatives may be evaluated by comparing information about the properties of each product and choosing to decide to buy from a variety of brand names to be left with only one brand that it may depend on the beliefs and beliefs in the brand, or may depend on the past consumer experience and the situation of the decision, as well as the available options. There are ideas to consider to help evaluate each option to make the decision easier as follows:

- Attributes and Benefit are the consideration of the benefits to be received and the properties of the product that what can be done or how talented? Each consumer will look at the product as a aggregate of various characteristics of the product, which consumers will look at the different characteristics of these characteristics as to how they relate to themselves, and they will pay the most attention to the characteristics associated with their needs.

- Degree of Importance is the consideration of the importance of the product (Attribute Importance) of the product rather than considering the outstanding product (Salient Attributes) that we have seen. Consumers pay more attention to various aspects of products at different levels according to their needs.

- Brand Beliefs is to consider the trust of the brand of the product or the image of the product (Brand Image) that consumers have seen and recognized from past experience. Consumers will create a belief in a brand of each brand's characteristics which the belief about branding has influenced the evaluation of consumer choices.

- Utility Function is to evaluate how satisfied is each product? Consumers have an attitude to choose a brand by the consumer will determine the product features that they want and then they will compare the features of the desired product with various brand features.

### 4) Purchase Decision

Normally, each consumer will need information and decision-making time for each product differently, some products require a lot of information and require a long comparison period, but some products, consumers do not need a long decision period.

### 5) Post-purchase Behaviour

After the purchase, consumers will gain experience in consumption which may be satisfied or not satisfied. If they are satisfied and aware of various advantages of the product, they will repeat purchases or may suggest new customers, but if they are not satisfied, they may stop buying that product in the next time and may adversely affect the following of customers to buy fewer products as well.

From the above, they describe consumer behavior related to the consumer purchasing decision process in 5 steps. In stage of the decision decisions, which is related to thought, feeling and action in the life of each human being who does not need to be the same. This is because each person has an attitude, motive, and stimuli in internal and external experiences. That actors will affect the feelings that lead to the purchasing decision process and after-purchase behavior.

## 2.4 INFORMATION ABOUT CULTURE IN AUSTRALIA

### The Cultural Aspect of Australia
### 2.4.1 Culture and Marketing

There is a relationship between content marketing and culture (Laroche, 2014, p. 921).Content marketing is a marketing approach that firms use to distribute valuable and relevant information about the brand to a specific target audience to stimulate interests from them. The information shared does not explicitly promote the brand. Its primary purpose is to create brand awareness or increased visibility. Through content marketing, it is possible to engage the target audience via digital marketing platforms. Companies develop educative, entertaining, engaging and compelling information to the audience. The success of content marketing lies on providing relevant information to the target audiences. Content marking often translates to profit, as it leads to more sales. Since content marketing needs a deeper understanding of the audience, it calls for more profound understanding of the culture of the audience. Mostly, the culture of the audience dictates behaviours of the audiences. According to Tenderich, (2014, p.23), spreadable content can only be attained through deeper understanding of the target audience and their cultures. There is no way a marketer can compose a successful message if the culture of the target audience is unknown. An effective content marketing must link with the emotions of the target audience. Culture includes ideas, and emotions that define that activities and the behaviour of the consumer. Different emotions and feelings are attached to a given culture, and therefore engaging the target audience emotionally needs a marketer to understand the cultural background of the target audience. For the story or the content to have an impact on the life of the audience, it must have a meaning. The content must have a meaning, and different cultures have different interpretation and attachment to a given story. A brand should appeal to the popular culture for effective interaction. Content marketing depends on the spreadability, made possible by the modern digital marketing platforms like Facebook. If an audience like the content, they would want to share with another person, who have the share the same culture. If the content does not match the culture of the audience, it will not be spread, as it will lack a story to connect them with the brand. The advert will be seen as irrelevant and not worthy of sharing with friends. On the worst, the content can be seen as offensive to a particular culture. If it is so, it will create a negative emotion, making the brand to be shared to criticize and condemning it. For a brand to be a success, the audience should feel part of it and have a connection.

## 2.4.2 Cultures in Australia

Due to globalization, international firms make everything possible to win customer loyalty from different regions of the world. These firms are faced with the problem of identifying and understanding the culture of the target audience. The Australian local firms have the same problem, as the country is heterogeneous culturally. Local firms try to win the majority of the population, but some miss the rest due to multicultural diversity. Every culture has different characteristics that make it difficult to engage them as a unit. The heterogeneity of culture in Australia is because of its migrant population, coming from different continents that do not share cultural dimensions (Wilkinson and Cheng, 2014, p. 106). In Australia, there as a sizable population of Chinese, Indians, Philippians, Britons, Aboriginals, African and others. Although the culture of a given community is dynamic, the Australia countries' background still has a greater effect since most of the migrant population were born outside Australia, and they speak another language than English. A person can learn about the behaviour and culture of a certain country by studying the advertisements only. This is because advertisements are conveying messages regarding the behaviour, norm, and interests of national culture (Makgosa, 2014, p. 360). It is a reflection of the countries believe and likes. In many advertisements, it is very easy to speculate on the issue of gender whether it is masculine of feminist's country. The advertisement must reflect what people believe in, and it is through this way that the country prides itself.

### 2.4.3 The Australian Set-up

Categorizing Australian culture based on Hofstede's cultural dimensions is complex. This is because the inhabitants are a mixture of varying cultures, some showing high power distance while other showing lower power distance. It is difficult to generalize the Australian cultural dimensions as each culture have different cultural dimensions, and the ability to react to an online advertisement is affected (Chan, 2015, p. 120). This means for effective advertisement and development of relationship marketing; each brand needs to approach the Australian market cautiously.

## 2.5 RELATED RESEARCH

Hernandez (2014) studied the website, important factors in e-business strategy, quality website design was part of an e-business strategy that became an important element for online marketing success. This article analyzied the main factors that must be taken into consideration when commercial website design. The purpose of this article was determination of important characteristics which must be taken into account in order to successfully design a commercial website. Case studies had been developed as research by Lin (2014) pointing out and analyzing Aceros de Spain company that analyzed customer perceptions to assess the quality of the website by focusing on analysis and development, update the website to make the business successful in the online market. From the results of the study, it found that the first important thing was the positioning of the tool to help find and facilitate access to the online market, the second was the speed of access to safety in shopping and security in payment. Importantly, do not disclose important information from customers in anyway. The last one was product information must be updated regularly and must be accurate, clear and important that meets the needs of customers. From this study showed that online marketing was successful, it must follow the website strategy as analyzed and used to develop the website for quality both in terms of simplicity but efficiency, and the speed of access to information.

Marko Merisavo (2014) studied the Effects of digital marketing on customer relationships. He stated that Viewing the use of digital channels in marketing from a customer relationship perspective offers several benefits to a marketer. Brand communication can be frequent and personalized, and different options for a dialogue exist. The benefits of dialogue include learning from and about customers, revealing their needs and interests, and being able to provide them with better and more personal service. From a customer perspective, the Internet has given power to get up-to-date information, to compare products and services more easily, and to get in touch with marketers. In a digital environment, customers increasingly use self- service and have more options to initiate action. A customer's perceived value of using digital channels and interacting with a marketer can come in several ways; it could be money, time, information, convenience, and so forth. This chapter examines how marketers can use digital channels to develop and strengthen customer relationships. In our framework, brand communication, service, personalization, and interactivity are suggested to be the key elements.

Suratcha Cherdbunmueang (2014) studied marketing factors and purchasing behaviors through electronic commerce among consumers in Bangkok. The research result of market factors that effected to the decision making on purchasing behaviors through electronic commerce showed the component as a group to focus on the security of database, a group to focus on the simplicity and modern, a group to focus on an importance of the returned-product and the quality of product, a group to focus on the communication through media, and finally was a group to focus on the advice and answers of the questions.

Athi Thammchiwa (2014) studied the influence of mobile marketing with social media on consumer behavior in Bangkok. With the purpose of education was (1) study motivation in various fields which was suitable for marketing through social media of Thai people (2) studying factors that influenced mobile marketing with effective social media in Bangkok. According to study, it found that the target group had experience related to mobile marketing with social media in the past 3 months, consumers still had a better understanding of mobile marketing with negative social media and still did not give feedback and did not trust in the information received through marketing in this channel. The important thing to help increasing consumer participation in marketing via mobile social media was content that matched the interests of consumers and the advice of friends to use this marketing tool sales promotion tends to be more successful than advertising.

Chonnikan Chulamakorn (2014) studied influential factors in behavior of purchasing goods via Internet of undergraduate students, faculty of Sciece, Burapha University. The results of this study are as follows: 1) There was only one personal factor, department, was not relating to influential factors about purchasing goods via internet. 2) There was only one factor about internet behavior, product, was not relating to influential about purchasing goods via Internet. 3) There are different means of score about influential factors about purchasing goods via internet for product and promotion between male andfemale students. 3.1) There are different means of score about influential factors about purchasing goods via internet for every sides among student years. 3.2) There are different means of score about influential factors about purchasing goods via internet for product among students which have different average income per month. 3.3) There are different means of score about influential factors about purchasing goods via internet for price among student which have different means of time for using internet.

Lindsey Julian (2014) studied using social media to increase consumer loyalty to a brand. With the increasing trend in the utilization of social media practices in the fields of public relations and marketing, it is becoming significantly important to understand how to effectively reach and communicate with consumers through this medium. This study focuses on the necessary tools, tactics, and strategies that should be utilized through social media in order to increase consumer loyalty.

Arun Srisiriwongchai (2014) studied a research on the role of digital media in the marketing strategy of luxury brands in Thailand which aimed to study the role and importance of digital media in the marketing strategy of the high fashion brands of the domestic market. The results of the research showed that (1) digital media was considered a medium that had played a role in creating a high-fashion brand marketing strategy for expansion, which could be an additional communication channel that could be done in conjunction with the communication strategy in the media. (2) high fashion brand customers were interested in acquiring information about fashion brands through digital media which was a communication that made customers more confident when buying those products. However, digital media could not be an incentive to buy such products through the online platform.

Jae Chun Liu (2014) studied the effectiveness of digital marketing communications with the Burberry brand in the People's Republic of China by surveying the opinions and attitudes of 216 Chinese consumers towards the Burberry brand. The survey results showed that using digital marketing strategies succeeded in creating awareness in the product well and helping to create channels more communication between the product and the consumer. However, the alleged strategy had no effect on increasing sales. This was because the decision to buy high-end fashion products had other elements that determine the behavior of consumers buying products.

Natthasak Worawittananon (2014) studied the attitude of consumers towards businesses selling products and services online. The study indicated that consumers' attitudes towards the business of selling products and online service before making a purchase that had the overall score at a moderate level ($\overline{X}$ = 3.16). When considering each aspect, it was found that personal information and product were at high level of attitude. In terms of payment channels and service were at moderate attitude. For the consumer's attitude towards businesses selling products and services online after the overall purchase decision was at a high level ($\overline{X}$ = 4.05). When considering each aspect, it was found that personal information, products and payment channels were at a high level of opinions. In terms of service, there was at moderate level of attitudes. The overall attitude of consumers towards businesses of selling products and services via online was different with statistical significance at .05 level.

Pawut Bunnark (2014) studied online business marketing strategy and usage behavior towards social; networks a case study of Facebook fanpage, Bangkok Metropolitan Area. The results showed that the most people who use Facebook Fanpage in Bangkok have experience for using Facebook Fanpage more than 4 years by using the Smartphone. The users purchase products from social networks, most are concerned about the quality of products with affordable prices because they cannot see the actual product and ensure the protection of customer information. However, such a some of user that order by the online, still has confidence and that if there is a call or payment by credit card. Shipping is quick and has a clearly stated price, quality and includes great after sale service. And organizing online stores to help consumers with the confidence and a better attitude to On-line shopping.

Afrina Yasmin, Sadia Tasneem, Kaniz Fatema (2015) studied effectiveness of digital marketing in the challenging age: an empirical study

by focusing on the importance of digital marketing for both marketers and consumers. They examine the effect of digital marketing on the firms' sales. Additionally the differences between traditional marketing and digital marketing in this paper are presented. This study has described various forms of digital marketing, effectiveness of it and the impact it has on firm's sales. The examined sample consists of one hundred fifty firms and fifty executives which have been randomly selected to prove the effectiveness of digital marketing. Collected data has been analyzed with the help of various statistical tools and techniques.

Bunga Chaisuwan and Methawee Jareunphon (2015) studied L'Officiel Thailand online marketing strategies. This research has found the online marketing strategies of L'Officiel Thailand to comprise four stages: 1) analysis of changing market situation; 2) classification of teenagers as a target group in addition to the main target group; 3) determination of online marketing strategies (e.g. strategy for the selection of channel, strategy for the timely and highly frequent presentation of contents, strategy for communication through brand ambassadors and beauty bloggers, strategy for online marketing budgeting, and, strategy for online marketing duration planning); and, 4) evaluation of L'Officiel Thailand with involvement of the target groups. The online marketing strategies are found to have improved the understanding of readers where contents and presentation of the magazine is concerned. Facebook is the most popular channel as it is most consistent with the daily routine of the readers. As for the readers, they are satisfied with and interested in real-time fashion contents which consequently leads to the behavior where they dress the way artists, stars and brand ambassadors do. This affects how they participate in activities ofthe magazine, purchase the magazine and subscribe to the magazine as well.

Charles Rupin (2015) studied social media as a new engaging channel in brands' relationship marketing. The objective of that research paper is to notice the changes brought by social media in brands relationship marketing. Also, it aims to see how relationship marketing changed over the years and what differs from traditional approaches marketers had. Moreover, this paper's purpose is to see how social media changed the way brands act toward customers and how customers gained power in their relationships with brands.

Phattharawadee Reanmanee (2015) studied digital integrated marketing communication to affecting the service boxing in Bangkok. The result revealed 1) the respondents agree with the Digital Integrated Marketing Communication, which were 1) Digital Advertising 2) Digital Personal Selling 3) Digital Sale Promotion 4) Digital Publicity and Public Relation 5) Digital Direct Marketing, 2) The result of the decision-making of client to Boxing in Bangkok Found that opinions on the decision. In most agree. And 3) the Digital Integrated Marketing Communication influenced the decision-making of client to use Boxing in Bangkok in the term of, Digital Advertising, Digital Personal Selling, Digital Publicity and Public Relation, Digital Direct Marketing with a statistical significance of 0.05.

Jidapha Tudhorm (2015) studied social media marketing, trust and information system quality affecting products' purchase decision through Facebook Live of online customers in Bangkok. The results showed that the factors affecting products' purchase decision through Facebook Live of customers in Bangkok with statistically significant at .05were social media marketing in terms of entertainment, trust, and information system quality in terms of information and service quality. These factors explained 67.8% of the influence on products' purchase decision through Facebook Live of customers in Bangkok. However, the social media marketing in terms of interaction, trendiness, customization, word of mouth, and the information system quality in terms of information quality did not affect through Facebook Live of customers in Bangkok.

Karnpat Leksrisakul (2015) studied the development of marketing strategy and marketing communication under marketing 3.0 concept of Hi-Q Product Foods Company Limited.

According to the result of the Study, during 1976-1986, the Company was owned by members of family, carried upon the businesses based upon Marketing 1.0 Concept concentrating on production factor or product orientation during 1976-1986, whereby the form of business operation to utilize Marketing 1.0 Concept to adopt the marketing mix in assisting in sale of products. According to the marketing communications, there were merely the marketing promotion to assist in sale of products and merely use of media, for example, newspaper and television advertising to enable the consumers to know the brand only. During 1986-2015, the Company carried upon the business by using name "Hi-Q Product Foods Co. Ltd.," the Company operated the businesses under Marketing 2.0 Concept with 2 brands, namely, Roza and Hi-Q. The Company used the marketing strategies by determining the marketing position for both brands, Roza was primary brand and Hi-Q was secondary brand. The products were divided into 3 groups, namely, canned foods, seasoning sauces, and instant foods. The target market was determined by dividing market shares in accordance with level of nature of package in the strategies creating the Roza brand merely. According to the marketing communications, the advertising is the main medium to transmit the products' qualifications in conjunction with other media, such as radio, printing matter, advertising in magazine, movable outdoor advertising, advertising at the point of sale and purchase, and marketing activities via online social network under the brand "Roza." During 2005-2015, the Company carried on businesses in line with the Marketing 3.0 Concept and continuously ran the projects as responsible for society, and mission, vision, and organizational good will were determined under the Marketing 3.0 Concept. Nonetheless, the Researcher found that, at present, Hi-Q Product Foods Co. Ltd. has simultaneously run the businesses in pursuance of the Marketing 2.0 Concept and the Marketing 3.0 Concept. The Marketing 2.0 Concept will focus on search for innovation to manufacture the products in response to the demands from consumers and continually operates the activities as responsible for society to create common social value simultaneously with the business operation.

Wipada Phittayawirut and Nak Gulis (2015) studied digital marketing influencing consumers' response in approaching marketing information. The results showed that most respondents were female, aged between 25 and 31, having status as single, holding bachelor's degree, working as private company employees, and earning average monthly income between 330$ and 670$. They have average frequency in using digital media to access the marketing information 4 days per week with 3 hours a day; Social media were mostly used; The reason for using digital media were convenience and rapidity; The digital media was used to be search engine and exchange products or services information; in the evening or early night from 6.01 p.m. to 12.00 p.m.; The respondents themselves mainly have an influence to use digital media in marketing information surfing. Consumers' perception toward market information was at the high levels. Consumers' lifestyle based on opinion was at the highest level, while their lifestyle based on interest and activity were at the high level. Consumers' responses based on overall were at the high levels. Consumers with different gender and education level influence response toward marketing information. Consumers' perception had the significant correlation to overall consumers' responses while lifestyle in category of average period in using digital media to access the marketing information per day and consumers' behavior in category of average frequency in using digital media had the significant correlation to consumers' responses in category of attention and desire.

Adiba Priyanka (2016) studied the role of digital branding on consumer retention: evaluating uses of social media in Bangladesh. The purpose of this paper is to evaluate social media on respect of digital branding and how it has helped the organizations to retain consumers in Bangladesh. Through this paper consumer retention was linked with various variables: Social Media Platform, Post Engagement, Purchase Behavior and Adverts on Social Media. Facebook is the most used platform in Bangladesh, which has been proved in this paper.

Discussion is done on how brand loyalty is directly linked to consumer retention.

Charinee Sanya and Pranee Aeimraorpakdee (2016) studied service marketing mix factors affecting the use of online banking transactions, Government Savings Bank in Chiang Rai Province

. From the research found that the majority of respondents were female . 69.50 per ,age 35-44 years old accounted for 74.80 percent of the bachelor's degree 77.30 percent , with a monthly income between 671$ to 1000$ or 38.80 percent had a career -employed / employed . 28.30 percent. Most of the service period of the customer with the bank for more than 10 percent to 48.50, the transaction is to take the money. 60.30 per cent during the service. Outside normal working hours of branches 38.75 per cent in the volume of services per month 1-4 times per month, representing 78.80 per cent had used online banking services. 63.50 percent. Attitude respondents have an understanding and knowledge about online banking. In most And reliability in the use of online banking and the use of online banking services at a high level. Demographic characteristics to the importance of the marketing mix of service users found that gender, age, occupation, income, education level. Important factors that affect the marketing mix (7Ps.). not different.

Kwan Phetsawang (2016) studied the possibility study of the strategic problems of the service infrastructure promotion from Thailand's digital economy policy. it is found that there are 63 main services currently provided to citizens. With the measurement of the online services, Thailand ranked lower in this index between 2012 to 2014. Moreover, it is indicated that many official websites contain a limited emerging information while the one stop services/portal and the smart card is still not effectively available. According to the Business Canvas model, there is a correspondence among various projects in terms of their operational procedures aimed at achieving the related national strategies and policies and clearly defined target group of each customer segment. However, it is suggested that there is no complete integration between the public services and its channel provided to citizens. It is an important issue as it leads to an economic efficiency in term of costs and benefits because the amount of public services provided through many channels at this time is inadequate to cover all necessary public services for citizens. Thus, they still have to practice as in the previous day to use those services, for example, they have to go to the places where public services are provided. Also, current public services do not cover all types of citizens, for example, the elderly and the disabled. The crucial reasons might be the limited number of cooperation among public services providers and the different readiness of each governmental offices in providing electronic services. Additionally, there is a restriction in the number of governmental officers working in information technology, information technology resources, and the revenue allocated for this digital economy plan. For policy recommendations, Thailand should accelerate the readiness among governmental offices in improving their electronic services for citizens through various channels. Also, this policy could be run on the basis of sustainable growth through supporting the necessary resources, for example, electronic infrastructures, specialists in information technology, and also the sufficient revenue in order to efficiently expand the number of electronic services to citizens thoroughly.

Prompan Tarnprasert (2016) studied the influence of digital marketing toward consumer's buying decision via e-commerce in Bangkok. The research's outcome has showed that samples were mostly female, 21-30years old, single status, bachelor degree, student and undergraduate, average monthly income 330$ - 670$ , hobby was surfing an internet, using ecommerce as a shopping channel to make a buying decision from its interesting promotion, made buying decision on their own, frequency 1-2 times per month with 20$ - 40$ each time, using shopping online to made a buying decision because it was convenience by 24 hours, using smartphone as a shopping's device between 16.01 - 20.00 and 20.01 – 24.00, shopping fashion products via Facebook. The hypothesis testing's result of digital marketing, website, marketing content, e-mail, front page, social media; had influence to consumer's buying decision towards ecommerce in Bangkok district at level of significant at 0.05.

Natthani Konghuayrob (2016) studied digital marketing communications influencing on Lazada website online buying behavior in Bangkok. The study revealed that most of sample group were female, aged 20-30, with a bachelor degree. They worked as employees and their average monthly incomes were 671$ - 1000$ per month. They bought online product in an average of 1-3 times in every 3 months and spent an average of 20$ - 40$ per purchase. Moreover, the main reasons of buying online products were product variety and convenience. Social media is the channel that made consumers recognize the products. In addition, once buying a product, consumers have high tendency to use the said website to purchase another or different product. In conclusion, digital marketing communications affected online buying behavior or consumers of Lazada website in Bangkok in purchase frequency, money spent on the purchase, and tendency to use the website again at 0.05 level of significance.

Bumrung Srinounpan and Chawanrat Tongchuay (2017) studied strategies using advertisement over the internet, to study about factors that using advertisement over the internet to make decision in business, study to the most suitable product for using advertisement over the internet, and study about the consumer behavior by using service over the internet. The results are: 1) There are two strategies using advertisement over the internet that have high score: beautiful and sharpen picture and text interesting 2) four factors have high score for decision using advertisement over the internet in business which are advertisement over the internet can be represent product data better than advertisement on paper, consumer can be searching data for support decision, present consumer behavior are different from the part, and in present product have short life cycle 3) four types of product have high score for using advertisement over the internet: software, book, service such as hotel, tourism, and costume 4) Instant message is the top service for consumer use over the internet such as MSN and ICQ, and search engine is secondary service.

Chombhak Klangrahad and Narapon Rurkoukos (2017) studied farmer's behavior in using social network for sale rice on Facebook website group type. a case study of group Facebook name " buy –sell rice for help farmers". The research found the reasons that Rice Farmers choose Facebook Website For buy Rice. First because this website is easly and convenienty to use and can connect directly to buyer target group. Second useing the facebook way can reduce trading time because the framers can deal directly with consumers in Facebook, This site is the fastest way to response consumer's questions and can send pictures of products via website. Last reason because Facebook is the most popular website its have many user in Thailand and Worldwide that make this site have wide range of users, Farmer can use it as advertising way. And use it for expand the consumer market to other target groups.

Guntalee Ruenrom (2017) studied the identification of research problems in digital marketing for Thailand in the future. It was found that both public and private sectors had great need of digital marketing research in order to help formulate the strategic goals, policies and guidelines for the development of Thai economy and the society under the rapidly changing environment in various perspectives more efficiently and effectively. The objective of this article was to identify the digital marketing research questions both macro and micro perspectives which match to the needs of Thailand in the future. Marketing and other related academicians can take the suggestions of digital research problems in various dimensions from this article and carry on the task of the digital marketing research that will benefit to the development of the economic and Thai society in the future.

Kedwadee Sombultawee (2017) studied analysis the tools of marketing communication affecting achievement Pong Hom Sri Jun brand of Thais teenagers in Bangkok. The results showed that the finding can group the market communication tools into 6 components which consisted of television ad media-printing, personal selling, digital media, marketing-activities media and outdoor media. All components can explain the variance of 74.57%. The contribution of this research can be used as a guide for improving and developing the marketing communications tools of Pong Hom Sri Jun brand to be effective and meet the consumers' needs.

Rakkwan Swarddipan (2017) studied marketing communication of Mono music by Youtube channel. The result of research is marketing communication of Mono Music by Youtube Channel have the best quality and the best feedback from the counting of views and subscribe on a music videos of artists by Youtube. The result is Youtube is the main channel for promoting music stuffs of Mono Music artists that have a highest feedback from a video stuffs like a long length music video and paid a high budget for the making production of music video that never have any music labels did and without a threat about media space that no more charge of continually within an official Youtube Channel of Mono Music that's make all artists and music stuffs of Mono Music become famous and get a good feedback from worldwide by Youtube media.

Somphob Adungjongrak (2017) studied marketing strategy of online products. The results found that 1) Finding indicated that overall area of purchasing behavior of consumers on online products were at very high level. However raking by mean first were type of products purchase (X=4.50) at very high level, selected brand name purchase (X= 4.19), purchasing frequency in 3 month ago (X=4.15), and purchasing expenditure in 3 month ago (X= 4.13) at high level respectively. 2) Finding indicated that overall area of significant level of factors lead to marketing strategy were at high level. However raking by mean first were logistics area (X= 4.06), place area X= 4.02), price area (X= 3.99), product area (X= 3.98), process area (X= 3.97), services provider (X= 3.96), marketing promotion X= 3.90) at high level respectively. 3) There were not significant different in significant level of factors lead to marketing strategy of customers classifier by gender, age, education attain, and average income per month 4) There were at moderate relationship level positive direction between overall area of significant level of factors lead to marketing strategy and purchasing behavior of online products consumers in term of purchasing expenditure in 3 month ago, purchasing frequency in 3 month ago, selected brand name purchase, and type of products purchase 5) Marketing strategy of online products = 863.46 logistics area +773 marketing promotion area +702.44 place area +650.18price area +609.55product area +391.45 service provider +357.23 process area.

Supot Gulati, Montri Verayankura, and Sirawit Sirirak (2017) studied causal of digital marketing influencing hotel customers' satisfaction and loyalty in the Andaman Triangle Cluster, Thailand. The causal study was found to be congruent with empirical data at a very good level in all hypotheses. In carrying out hypothesis testing, the researcher has concluded the following: (1) most customers were men ages between 26-41 years old with monthly income between

50,000 and 150,000. They were mostly educated couple travelers with bachelor degree from Europe (such as Sweden, Scandinavia, France, etc.), Malaysia and Singapore working in the private companies. They travel between 1-2 times a year, stay in the hotel within 1-5 days and booked their rooms through online travel agent (OTA), (2) website marketing can influence the hotel's customers to perceive the value of services of the hotel significantly (3) social media marketing and content marketing can directly influence the customers' loyalty on the services of the hotel (4) website marketing can influence the customers' satisfaction and loyalty, once the customers have perceived the value of services of the hotel (5) the customers' satisfaction can result to the customers' loyalty significantly. Therefore, the results can be summarized that the digital marketing and perceived value factors have direct and indirect influence towards the customers' satisfaction and loyalty significantly.

Tanakorn limsarun (2017) studied digital marketing communications toward taxi service applications in Bangkok, Thailand. The results of study have shown demographic data that the majority of samples were male, 18 – 25 years old, graduated in Bachelor's degree, private company employees, and average monthly income ranging from 330$ – 670$. The samples used taxi service application because they need the transportation service to their workplace, availability and ubiquitous service. While most of the samples used taxi service application 3 - 5 times per month and most of the service was on every Monday at 7am – 9am. Thus, the digital marketing communications have been related to the decision to used taxi service application in Bangkok Thailand as shown by a multiple linear regression equation. Decision Making Service = 0.394 Digital Media Promotion + 0.325 Perceptual + 0.297 Perceived Benefit - 0.104 Digital Advertising. Moreover, the consumer's decision to used taxi service application in Bangkok was effected by four aspects of the digital marketing communication at 68.5 percent in Bangkok was effected by four aspects of the digital marketing communication at 68.5 percent.

Wipada Amphai (2017) studied impact of social media used to create strategies for expanding opportunities and efficiency in small and medium enterprises. Research found that in Social Media use, main expectations of SMEs' owner-managers are to create effective business both in sale and branding, along with, to build good long-term relationship between business and consumers. Despite all that, it takes time and constantly effort to maintain such good service; in accordance with the least agreed comment given in this research, with 3.88 mean scores, that social media has an influence on keeping permanent bond with consumers, furthermore, there is concern of how information on social media spreads rapidly and widely and hard to control, and this could be either good or harmful effect for business. On the other hand, research found that prompt response via social media is highly satisfied by consumers, with .731 mean scores and the level of statistical significance found at 0.05.

Guntalee Ruenrom (2018) studied the identification of research problems in digital marketing for Thailand in the future. The study showed that Digital marketing is increasing its role and importance both in the operation of all type of businesses in all levels including the rise of impacts on the quality of life of consumers. Marketing academicians should be aware of the importance of the digital marketing research problem identification that must fit to the needs and providing benefits to the economic and Thai society in the future. Based on the analysis and the synthesis of the past research to the present in order to identify the state-of-the-art of the digital marketing research as well as the organized visionary meeting that digital experts from different professions were invited to share their visions for digital marketing in the future. It is found that both public and private sectors have great need of digital marketing research in order to help formulate the strategic goals, policies and guidelines for the development of Thai economy and the society under the rapidly changing environment in various perspectives more efficiently and effectively. The objective of this article is to identify the digital marketing research questions both macro and micro perspectives which match to the needs of Thailand in the future. Marketing and other related academicians can take the suggestions of digital research problems in various dimensions from this article and carry on the task of the digital marketing research that will benefit to the development of the economic and Thai society in the future.

# CHAPTER 3
# Dynamics of the Anticipated Solution

This chapter describes goals, objectives of investigation, and the method of research which uses both quantitative and qualitative approaches consisting of population and sample, research instrument, data collection , data analysis.

## 3.1 GOALS

The goal of digital marketing strategy is today's marketers who aim to use technology to help businesses grow rapidly with low cost, observation, experiment, and learning, the key of this goal is to be able to repeat which responds to the business which is highly competitive and wants to grow rapidly with the digital marketing strategy model, the main goal is to create a marketing machine that can bring or create customers. (In particular, this research is customers who are permanently in Australia). It make customers know about buying, reusing and telling in products or services with digital marketing channels that start from the design, development of products and services to get people to know. There are customers come to use the service, and then comes to let people use it repeatedly and continue to tell until the measure of income by adhering to the data analysis and insight processes, creating new ideas priority in the experiment and conducting experiments in order to observe and learn by means that can be measured and extended to get the best goals and ideas.

## 3.2 OBJECTIVES OF INVESTIGATION

The long-term aim of this research is to understand the relationships between the digital marketing techniques applied by the Australian firms or firms targeting the Australian audience and the culture of the audience. The objective of this study is to provide a comprehensive review of marketing industry practices and literature on the effects of cultures on digital marketing techniques. It will analyze modern digital marketing techniques applied by firms in Australia, technique effectiveness and assess whether these techniques are affected by the diversified culture in the Australian market. Specifically, this research has the following sub-objectives:

1) To study the problems and needs of the digital marketing strategy model that is suitable for culture in Australia.

2) To develop a digital marketing strategy that is suitable for culture in Australia.

3) To evaluate and confirm the appropriate digital marketing strategy model for culture in Australia.

## 3.3 POPULATION AND SAMPLE

This study comprised 400 people who were major nationalities and the ethnic background of Australians (18 years and above) in Sydney, Melbourne, Perth, Adelaide, Darwin, Brisbane, and Canberra that data was be collected top six multicultural cities as per 2016 census. Convenient sampling was be sued to find potential respondents that meet specific criteria. Convenient sampling also was known as accidental sampling was defined as a non-random sampling method where members of the population that met a particular criterion like age, accessibility, and willingness to participate. Formula of Yamane (2014) was used for determining the size of a sample.

3.3.1 The researcher has conducted the selection of the sample as follows:

3.3.1.1 Find the total number of population groups which is a consumer group in Sydney, Melbourne,

Perth, Adelaide, Darwin, Brisbane, and Canberra, number 5,696,409 people (Bureau of Registration Administration Department of Local Administration, Ministry of Interior, 2015)

3.3.1.2 Determine the sample size from Yamane's finished table (2014) and get 400 people.

3.3.1.3 Selecting samples by the Convenience Sampling method

3.3.1.4 Proportion of the number of samples is Internet users and 400 social networking users in Sydney, Melbourne, Perth, Adelaide, Darwin, Brisbane, and Canberra through 3 platforms, because Facebook is the most used. Line and Twitter that are ranked 6th. ("Reveal Internet usage statistics", 2016) as follows:

- Facebook group of 192 people using the Google form deposit method in the off-page of the electronic commerce business group.

- Line group of 168 people using Google form deposit with the shop group online with a channel to contact consumers via the line.

- Twitter groups 40 people using Google form via hashtags related to direct access to consumer groups.

Because there are 47 million Facebook users, LINE number 41 million, and Twitter 9 million ("ETDA reveals survey results", 2015)

## 3.4 RESEARCH INSTRUMENT

The researcher used the questionnaire as a tool to collect data from samples. The details of the questionnaire are as follows:

3.4.1   Study how to create questionnaires from research papers and related theories.

3.4.2   Create a questionnaire to ask for opinions on 3 different issues: (1) general information about respondents (2) behavior of buying products and services through e-commerce (3) opinions about digital marketing by dividing 5 digital marketing tools including websites, content marketing, email, search engine optimization and social media (4) comments about decisions to buy, and (5) other suggestions.

3.4.3   The questionnaire was created to be presented to the advisor. To improve

3.4.4   Making improvements and proposing to the advisor to verify the accuracy again for the advisor to approve before handing out the questionnaire

3.4.5   Take the questionnaire to experiment with 10 samples to find the confidence value.

3.4.6   Improve and propose to the advisor to approve before handing out the questionnaire.

3.4.7   Give away the questionnaire to the sample.

## 3.5 TOOL INSPECTION

<u>Content validation</u> The researcher presented a questionnaire that was created to the advisor to verify the completeness and consistency of the content of the questionnaire that matches the subject to be studied.

<u>Verification of confidence</u> The researcher considers Cronbach's Alpha Coefficient which has the following details:

### Table 3.1 : Showing the Cronbach Alpha coefficient, questions related to the behavior of buying products and services through e-commerce.

| Part of Questions | Alpha values (show confidence) | |
| --- | --- | --- |
| | Experimental group (N = 30) | Sample group (N = 400) |
| Digital Market | | |
| - Website | 0.619 | 0.726 |
| - Content Market | 0.753 | 0.789 |
| - E-Mail Marketing | 0.792 | 0.790 |
| - Search Engine Optimization | 0.710 | 0.725 |
| - Social Media | 0.896 | 0.839 |
| Developing an appropriate digital marketing strategy model for culture in Australia | 0.820 | 0.757 |

Criteria for determining Cronbach's alpha coefficients ($\alpha$) are between $0 < \alpha < 1$. The results of the confidence test showed that the reliability of the questionnaire when applied to the experimental sample. There were 30 samples and 400 samples of questionnaires with the reliability of the questionnaire. The question in each variable has a confidence level between 0.619 - 0.896 which results of Cronbach's alpha coefficient of both samples. (Nunnally, 2014).

## 3.6 QUESTIONNAIRE ELEMENTS

The researcher issued a questionnaire consisting of 5 parts, along with the following methods of answering questions:

Part 1 is a question about general information of respondents, including gender, age, status, education level, occupation and average monthly income. The question is a closed-ended question to choose from.

Part 2 is a question related to the behavior of choosing to buy products and services through the e-commerce business.

Part 3 is a question related to opinions about digital marketing by dividing 5 digital marketing tools including websites, content marketing, email, search engine optimization and social media.

Part 4 is a question related to opinions about digital marketing with culture in Australia

Part 5 is a question related to other suggestions. Appearance is an open-ended question.

## 3.7 DATA COLLECTION

The researcher has collected data according to the following steps:

### Qualitative Methods

In-depth interviews was conducted with the target Australian persons by selecting 5 males and 5 females: total 10 people from various age, occupation, education, income, and nationality. The collected information was focused on their feedback regarding the electronic commerce business from the structure interview that was conducted by using open-ended questions relating to questions as follows:

1) Profile of key informant (gender, age, occupation, education, income, and nationality)

2) Why do you choose to buy products through the electronic commerce business?

3) What do your opinions about digital marketing by dividing 5 digital marketing tools including websites, content marketing, email, search engine optimization and social media?

4) How long do you take to buy products via electronic commerce business?

## Quantitative Methods

Step 1 The researcher requests cooperation and explains the details of the content within the questionnaire including how to respond to respondents.

Step 2 Researchers conduct online questionnaires posted on social networks that are defined as Facebook, Line and Twitter, and send to respondents.

Step 3 Collect the questionnaire and evaluate the number of queries returned that there is a complete and complete number of designs that are 400 sets or not.

## 3.8 THE INTERPRETATION OF DATA

According to Miah (2014) a five-scale interval was used to measure the degree of using digital marketing from 1.00-5.00 values. The five scales comprises of very low, low, moderate, high and very high. The value of each scale was assigned as follows.

| Very Low | Low | Moderate | High | Very High |
|----------|-----------|-----------|-----------|-----------|
| 1.00-1.49 | 1.50-2.49 | 2.50-3.49 | 3.50-4.49 | 4.50-5.00 |

The score of above items could be calculated by using the following formula.

WAI = [fVh (1.0) + fH (0.8) + fM (0.6) + fL(0.4) +fV1 (0.2)] / N

When, WAI = Weighted Average Index

fVh= Frequency of very high

fH = Frequency of high

fM = Frequency of medium

fL = Frequency of low

fV1= Frequency of very low

N = Total number of observation

## 3.9 DATA ANALYSIS

The researcher has set the statistics for data analysis.

### 3.9.1 Qualitative Analysis

Qualitative statement was used to describe the In-depth interviews that was conducted with the target Australian persons by selecting 5 males and 5 females from various occupations. The information collected was focused on their feedback regarding the electronic commerce business.

### 3.9.2 Quantitative Analysis

3.9.2.1 Descriptive statistics explains general information and qualifications of participants in gender, age, status, education level, occupation and income per month.

3.9.2.2 Reference statistic analyzes comparison and analysis of data related to variables in the study as follows:

- Hypothesis uses multiple regression statistics to analyze the influence of digital marketing strategy development on the cultures in Australia.

# CHAPTER 4
# Overall Outcomes

This chapter were a data analysis for explaining and testing hypotheses related to each variable. For qualitative method, the researcher used statement that was used to describe the In-depth interviews of key informant interviews. For quantitative method, the researcher collected data from questionnaires with complete answers (total 400 sets: 100% of the total number of 400 questionnaires. The researchers reported using descriptive statistics and using multivariate statistics for data analysis. The analysis of the data must be in accordance with the preliminary agreement. The researcher presented the results of the analysis into 3steps, respectively,

4.1    Strategy and Techniques

4.2    Statement of key informant interviews.

4.3    Descriptive Statistics: Frequency, Percentage, Mean and Standard Deviation.

4.4    Inferential Statistics: The analysis of hypotheses by using multiple regression statistics

4.5    Conclusion

## 4.1 STRATEGY AND TECHNIQUES

Digital strategy and marketing techniques are marketing through electronic devices by using the computer or smartphone that is the information that is sent to consumers which can track the response in a short time. Most of the digital marketing often comes in the form of campaigns or advertisements which has been very popular with today's marketers. There are 5 digital strategies and marketing techniques to be used as a guideline for creating digital strategies as follows:

1. Create a buyer persona

Before creating a marketing strategy, whether online or offline what should be done is to create a buyer persona to learn about buyer behavior, and used to plan the strategy in marketing to the point as well as determining the digital marketing strategy that comes from the details of the buyer, the buyer you have set up will be represented as a representative for most customers. The researcher can create the identity of the buyer from the survey, interviewing the target groups that have been defined and used to make assumptions without distorting the information obtained from the survey or interviews to prevent errors in information that will adversely affect marketing strategies.

2. Identify your digital marketing goals and tools.

The marketing goals created should be linked to business goals such as setting a business goal that will increase revenue for online businesses by 20% within 1 year. The goal as a marketer is to increase sales opportunities by more than 50% within 1 year. These two parts are targeted at relevance and affect each other. When there is a goal, it is necessary to have a method or tools for measuring results which method of measurement or the effectiveness of digital marketing. There are different forms depending on the goal and business model for tools that can be used to measure digital marketing that can be easily used, namely Hubspot software for digital marketing that is responsible for collecting information In trading that is expressed as the value of statistics that can be accurately measured.

3. Evaluate digital marketing channels and funds

Evaluate the digital marketing channels of how much content is available for managing strategy based on the digital media brand whether it is a website, business profile, networks based on social networks, blogs and other content that can be controlled including content from outside the website that is not displayed on the website as well.

### 4. Check and plan advertising media own

The heart of digital marketing is the proprietary media. Most of the media are in the form of content as well as various messages that is published in your brand name whether it's the first page of the website, like the about us page, product descriptions, various posts within the blog or social media is considered the same content, so all you have to do is check the media or content on the online world that is suitable for advertising or attract the attention of those who see or content that will help you achieve your goals and bring those content as part of your advertising plan to increase your sales opportunities.

### 5. Check and plan the advertising media receiving

Evaluating the media previously received with your current goals will help to know which direction to focus on from viewing the traffic details of the audience that comes into your website, where it comes from, which links, which visitors click to enter your website to find effective links as well as finding content or the most quality pages. It can check this information by using a good Google Analytics tool from Google that is free to use or choosing other tools according to your own needs based on the information that obtained, it will be able to plan, change strategy, or correct errors in a timely manner.

In sum, using digital techniques and strategies as a marketing tool considering that the selection of strategies that are suitable for the current consumer behavior.

## 4.2 GENERAL INFORMATION OF KEY INFORMANTS

There were ten key informants who were Australian persons by selecting 5 males and 5 females from various occupations as followed:

The researcher synthesized the details from the interview as shown in the following interview:

## (1) Profile of key informant (gender, age, occupation, education, income, and nationality)

" I'm 21 years old. My nationality is Thai. I have just graduated from university in bachelor degree. I am waiting the interview result at private company. I get 445 dollar per month from my parents. " (The 1st female persons, 2018)

" I'm 30 years old. I'm Chinese. I graduated in bachelor degree. I'm private company employee. I get 888 dollar per month from there." (The 2nd female persons, 2018)

" I'm 29 years old. I'm Aboriginals. I graduated in bachelor degree. I'm government official. I get 500 dollar per month. " (The 3rd female persons, 2018)

" I'm 35 years old. I'm Filipino. I am studying in Master degree. I get 600 dollar per month from my parents" (The 4th female persons, 2018)

" I'm 23 years old. I'm Indian. I am studying in Master degree. I get around 500 dollar per month from my part-time job." (The 5th female persons, 2018)

" I'm 29 years old. I'm Briton. I graduated in bachelor degree. I'm private company employee. I get 888 dollar per month from there." (The 6th male persons, 2018)

" I'm 25 years old. I'm Thai. I am studying in Master degree. I get 445 dollar per month from my parents, and around 200 dollar form part-time job. " (The 7th male persons, 2018)

" I'm 32 years old. I'm African. I graduated in bachelor degree. I'm private company employee. I get 800 dollar per month from there." (The 8th male persons, 2018)

" I'm 32 years old. I'm Filipino. I graduated in bachelor degree. I'm private company employee. I get 800 dollar per month from there." (The 9th male persons, 2018)

" I'm 28 years old. I'm Chinese. I graduated in bachelor degree. I'm private company employee. I get 885 dollar per month from there." (The 10th male persons, 2018)

From the interview, it can be concluded that the answer of the persons in Australia show that there are different culture in Australia because there are many nationalities who live in Australia. For education, they graduated bachelor's degree. For age, they are around 21-35. For occupation, they are students, private company employee, and government official. For monthly income, they get around 444-888 dollar.

## (2) Why do you choose to buy products through the electronic commerce business?

" I'm satisfied with the purchase of products through the digital marketing because I always search for information or reviews of products of my culture from the Internet to help in making a purchase decision, and I will introduce the products to others in my culture and want to come back to buy again." (The 1st female persons, 2018)

" I choose to buy products through the digital marketing because I meet the needs and convenience for my culture." (The 2nd female persons, 2018)

" I can take time to compare product information in qualification, reliable, price and promotion to choose the best option for me. " (The 3rd female persons, 2018)

" I like to search for information or reviews of products in my culture from the Internet to help in making a purchase decision, and it' safe for me to buy product from digital market." (The 4th female persons, 2018)

" I am interested in seeing advertisements or product promotions through various social media, and I often get benefits through email and I am impressed." (The 5th female persons, 2018)

" It is comfortable for me because I can buy and take time to choose the products everywhere in the world, Moreover, I can communicate quickly and interact with the store easily." (The 6th male persons, 2018)

" I feel safe when I find the shop on the first page, I feel the shop that is credible, and I can read the review of the products from my culture" (The 7th male persons, 2018)

" I choose to buy products through the digital marketing because you meet the needs and convenience for my culture " (The 8th male persons, 2018)

" I'm always interested in graphics that are short, concise and easy to understand on the Internet when I want to buy something. I believe that the content on the Internet are reliable because there are a lot review from consumers in different culture." (The 9th male persons, 2018)

" I always receive an email with news or promotions and are interested, and I often get benefits through email. Moreover, I like to shop with digital market because I always meet the needs for my culture." (The 10th male persons, 2018)

From the interview, it can be concluded that the answer of the persons in Australia show that each culture in Australia is different, and the ability to react to an online advertisement is affected in purchasing.

### (3) What do your opinions about digital marketing by dividing 5 digital marketing tools including websites, content marketing, email, search engine optimization and social media?

" For website, I often visit the store's main website to buy products because it's safe. For content, I'm always interested in graphics that are short, concise and easy to understand. For email, I like it because I always receive an email with news or promotions and are interested. For search engine optimization, when I find the shop on the first page, I felt the shop that is credible. For social media, I feel that social media is a way to update convenient and fast information." (The 1st female persons, 2018)

" For website, I think that buy products on websites that are easy to use, and do not complex. For content, I am always interested in content that has both content and entertainment. I'm always interested in graphics that are short, concise and easy to understand. For email, I like it because I often receive information about the product and purchase; especially, discount and promotion. For search engine optimization, when I find the shop on the first page, I felt the shop that is credible. For social media, I feel that social media is a way to update convenient and fast information." (The 2nd female persons, 2018)

" For website, I like to click the banner ad to access the homepage of the website, and choose to buy products because it is easy for choosing. For content, I like graphics that are short and easy to understand. For email, I like it because I often receive promotion and can communicate quickly and interact with the store easily. For search engine optimization, when I find the shop on the first page, I felt the shop that is credible. For social media, I feel that social media is a way to update convenient and fast information." (The 3rd female persons, 2018)

" For website, I believe that products on websites are reliable, but they have to be on the first page of Google. For content, I am always interested in content that provides useful information about products, but I don't want to read only letters but also communicating with images or storytelling with pictures. For email, I like it because I often receive promotion and can communicate quickly and interact with the store easily. For search engine optimization, when I find the shop on the first page, I felt the shop that is credible. For social media, I feel that social media is a way to update convenient and fast information." (The 4th female persons, 2018)

" For website, I feel safe if I visit the store's main website to buy products. For content, I am always interested in content that provides useful information about products, and I am often interested in communicating with images or storytelling with pictures. For email, I often receive promotion and can communicate quickly and interact with the store easily. For search engine optimization, when I find the shop on the first page, I felt the shop that is credible. I always find the products from the first page of Google. For social media, I feel that social media is a way to update convenient and fast information." (The 5th female persons, 2018)

" For website, I like to click the banner ad to access the homepage of the website, and choose to buy products. For content, I am always interested in content that provides useful information about products, and I am interested in graphics that are short, concise and easy to understand. For email, I often receive promotion and can communicate quickly and interact with the store easily. For search engine optimization, when I find the shop on the first page, I felt the shop that is credible. I always find the products from the first page of Google. For social media, I feel that social media is a way to update convenient and fast information, and are the good way for buying decision." (The 6th male persons, 2018)

" For website, I will focus the homepage of the website, and choose to buy products that have sharing for checking comments about products that I want. For content, I think that in graphics, image help to easy to understand because sometimes I can't understand some language in the content, so graphics, image and storytelling with pictures can help me to understand about the products. For email, I like it because I always receive a lot promotion and can communicate quickly and interact with the store easily. For search engine optimization, when I find the shop on the first page, I felt the shop that is credible; especially, the shops that are on the first of Google. For social media, I feel that social media is always update information, so I like to search the products on social media " (The 7th male persons, 2018)

"For website, I always access the homepage of the website from my friends' recommendation or sharing. For content, I like content that provides useful information about products including graphics and image that are easy to understand. For email, I like it because I always receive a lot extra promotion from it. For search engine optimization, I like to find the shop on the first page of Google because I feel that the shops on the first page dare to invest for customers to see their products, and when I find the shop on the first page, I feel the shops that are credible. For social media, I feel that social media is always update information about products that I want."(The 8th male persons, 2018)

"For website, I like to access the homepage of the website from my friends' suggestions because my friends who introduce website to me are satisfied with the products from that website, so I believe that I will not waste of time to find website by myself. For content, I like content that provides useful information about products including graphics and images that are easy to understand. I always receive extra information about the product and purchase via email. For search engine optimization, I think it is important for me that I don't want to waste of time for searching, so I believe that the information that are on the first page are the most interesting. For social media, I choose to buy the products from social media because it is always update information about product and it is easy to ask and get information from it." (The 9th male persons, 2018)

" I always visit the website from the reviews of my cultural because it help me to meet the right product to be suit with me, and the content in the website should be useful information about products including graphics and images that are easy to understand. For email, I like it because I always receive a lot discount from it. For search engine optimization, the first page of Google is always searched by me because I feel that are credible. I like to shop on social media because it is always update information about products that I want, and when I follow various social fan pages, I can receive fast information." (The 10th male persons, 2018)

From the interview, it can be concluded that the answer of the persons who are different cultural in Australia show that websites, content marketing, email, search engine optimization and social media influence each culture in Australia in purchasing such as (1) For website, they often visit the store's main website to buy products, they often buy products on websites that are easy to use, and do not complex, they often buy products on websites that are reliable, they often click the banner ad to access the homepage of the website, and choose to buy products. (2) For content marketing, (1) they are always interested in content that provides useful information about product. (2) they are often interested in communicating with images or storytelling with pictures. (3) they are always interested in graphics that are short, concise and easy to understand. (4) they are always interested in content that has both content and entertainment. For e-mail, (1) they receive an email with news or promotions and are interested. (2) they get benefits through email and are impressed. (3) they receive information about the product and purchase via email. (4) they can communicate quickly and interact with the store easily. For search engine optimization, (1) when searching for a store, they usually click to enter the store's first address. (2) when you find the shop on the first page, they felt the shop that is credible. (3) they often choose to click a website with short web names / easy to understand and enter only important word. (4) they often choose to click on websites that have advertisements on websites (Search Engine like Google). For social marketing, (1) they often click to follow various social fan pages to receive information of store. (2) they feel that social media is a way to update convenient and fast information. (3) they are interested in seeing advertisements or product promotions through various social media. (4) they often use social media to find information and buy product.

### (4) How long do you take to buy products via electronic commerce business?

" I think not more than an hour to buy products via electronic commerce business. " (The 1st female persons, 2018)

" I think not more than 30 minutes to buy products via electronic commerce business." (The 2nd female persons, 2018)

" May be 30 minutes or an hour depend on product " (The 3rd female persons, 2018)

" Normally, I use 30- 1 hour. Sometimes I take 1-2 days to decide buying product via electronic commerce business." (The 4th female persons, 2018),

" Not more than an hour for buying products via electronic commerce business. " (The 5th female persons, 2018)

" I sometimes use 30 minutes, but normally, it is not less than 30 minutes." (The 6th male persons, 2018)

" Only 30 - 1 hour to decide buying products via electronic commerce business. " (The 7th male persons, 2018)

" Depend on product, I never decide to buy more than a day. " (The 8th male persons, 2018)

" Not more than an hour to buy product via electronic commerce business." (The 9th male persons, 2018)

" Every products on digital market, I never decide to buy them more than a day." (The 10th male persons, 2018)

From the interview, it can be concluded that the answer of the persons in Australia show that the ability to buy is fast because most of them use time for buying decisions not more than a day, but there is only one answer that show may use 2 days for buying decision. I think that it is because of her age and her experience.

## 4. 3 GENERAL INFORMATION OF THE RESPONDENTS ( DESCRIPTIVE STATISTICS)

Table 4.3.1: To show frequency and percent from general information of the respondents.

| Variable | Frequency | Percent |
|---|---|---|
| **1. Gender** | | |
|     Male | 98 | 24.50 |
|     Female | 302 | 75.50 |
| Total | 400 | 100 |
| **2. Age** | | |
|     Lower or Equal 20 | 99 | 24.8 |
|     21-30 | 205 | 51.20 |
|     31-40 | 62 | 15.50 |
|     41-50 | 23 | 5.80 |
|     51 or over | 11 | 2.80 |
| Total | 400 | 100 |
| **3. Marital status** | | |
|     Single | 350 | 87.50 |
|     Married | 44 | 11.00 |
|     Divorced / widowed | 6 | 100 |
| Total | 400 | 100 |
| **4. Education Level** | | |
|     Lower than high school | 30 | 7.50 |
|     High school | 72 | 18.00 |
|     Diploma or equivalent | 18 | 4.50 |
|     Bachelor's Degree | 236 | 59.50 |
|     Master's Degree | 43 | 10.80 |
|     Ph.D. | 1 | 0.30 |
| Total | 400 | 100 |

## Table 4.3.1: To show frequency and percent from general information of the respondents. (to continue)

| Variable | Frequency | Percent |
|---|---|---|
| **5. Occupation** | | |
| Student | 156 | 78.4 |
| Business owner / freelance | 54 | 11.4 |
| Private company employees | 142 | 2.5 |
| State enterprise employees / government officials | 25 | 3.4 |
| Housewife / butler | 9 | 1.3 |
| Other | 14 | 3.50 |
| Total | 2 | 0.8 |
| **6. Average monthly income** | | |
| Lower or equal 444 dollar | 141 | 35.30 |
| 444-888 dollar | 151 | 37.80 |
| 888-1332 dollar | 68 | 17.00 |
| 1,332-1,776 dollar | 13 | 3.30 |
| 1,776-2,220 dollar | 11 | 2.80 |
| 2,219 or over dollar | 16 | 4.00 |
| Total | 400 | 100 |
| **7. Hobbies** | | |
| Surfing the Internet | 182 | 45.50 |
| Shopping | 26 | 6.50 |
| Watching movie/ Listening to music | 98 | 24.50 |
| Reading | 25 | 6.30 |
| Playing sports/ games | 41 | 10.30 |
| Pet | 15 | 3.80 |
| Other | 13 | 3.30 |
| **8. Nationality (Makgosa, 2012, p. 360).** | | |
| Chinese | 182 | 45.50 |
| Indians | 26 | 6.50 |
| Philippians | 98 | 24.50 |
| Britons | 25 | 6.30 |
| Aboriginals | 41 | 10.30 |
| African | 15 | 3.80 |
| Other | 13 | 3.30 |
| Total | 400 | 100 |

## 4.3.2 Information on the behavior of buying products and services through the electronic commerce business that shows the amount and percentage ( Descriptive Statistics)

## Table 4.3.2: To show frequency and percent from the behavior of buying products and services through the electronic commerce business.

| Variable | Frequency | Percent |
|---|---|---|
| **9. The reason you decide to buy products or services through electronic commerce business.** | | |
| Others persuade | 26 | 6.5 |
| There are interesting promotional items. | 163 | 40.80 |
| Cheaper than the general market | 123 | 30.80 |
| Confident in the safety system | 51 | 12.80 |
| Other | 37 | 9.30 |
| Total | 400 | 100 |
| **10. Persons influencing the decision to purchase products or services through electronic commerce business.** | | |
| Decide for yourself | 278 | 69.50 |
| Family members | 27 | 6.80 |
| Friends / colleagues | 28 | 7.00 |
| Famous person | 10 | 2.50 |
| Notice from those who were used that product or service before. | 57 | 14.20 |
| Other | 0 | 0.00 |
| Total | 400 | 100 |
| **11. Frequency of buying products or services through commercial businesses electronics per month** | | |
| Not more than 1 times | 145 | 36.30 |
| 1 – 2 times | 182 | 45.50 |
| 3 – 4 times | 47 | 11.80 |
| 5 – 6 times | 16 | 4.00 |
| 7 or more 7 times | 10 | 2.50 |
| Total | 400 | 100 |

## Table 4.3.2: To show frequency and percent from the behavior of buying products and services through the electronic commerce business.

| Variable | Frequency | Percent |
|---|---|---|
| **12. The price of products or services that are purchased via the electronic commerce business per times.** | | |
| Not more than 22 dollar | 130 | 32.50 |
| 23 - 45 dollar | 172 | 43.00 |
| 46 – 67 dollar | 59 | 14.80 |
| 68 or more 68 dollar | 39 | 9.80 |
| Total | 400 | 100 |
| **13. The most reason for choosing to buy products or services through the electronic commerce business.** | | |
| Cheaper than general market buying. | 61 | 15.30 |
| Need convenience because of buying 24 hours. | 199 | 49.80 |
| Available in a variety of normal rather than buying in general market. | 72 | 18.00 |
| Can study opinions from those who have used the service before. | 61 | 15.30 |
| Other | 7 | 1.80 |
| Total | 400 | 100 |
| **14. The most frequently used equipment to access the electronic commerce business.** | | |
| Smartphone | 349 | 87.30 |
| Notebook/ PC | 37 | 9.30 |
| Tablet | 14 | 3.50 |
| Other | 0 | 0.00 |
| Total | 400 | 100 |

## Table 4.3.2: To show frequency and percent from the behavior of buying products and services through the electronic commerce business.

| Variable | Frequency | Percent |
|---|---|---|
| **15. During the time that using the Internet to purchase goods or services.** | | |
| 04.01– 08.00 | 1 | 0.30 |
| 08.01 – 12.00 | 23 | 5.80 |
| 12.01 – 16.00 | 63 | 15.80 |
| 16.01 – 20.00 | 154 | 38.50 |
| 20.01 – 24.00 | 154 | 38.50 |
| 00.01 – 04.00 | 5 | 1.30 |
| Total | 400 | 100 |
| **16. Types of products or services that are most frequently purchased via electronic commerce.** | | |
| Fashion products | 182 | 45.50 |
| Health and Beauty Products | 98 | 24.50 |
| IT equipment | 46 | 11.50 |
| Household | 24 | 6.00 |
| Travel / Tourism | 19 | 4.80 |
| Other | 31 | 7.80 |
| Total | 400 | 100 |
| **17. Channels of e-commerce businesses used to purchase products or services.** | | |
| Website | 110 | 27.50 |
| Facebook | 123 | 30.80 |
| Line | 19 | 4.80 |
| Instagram | 84 | 21.00 |
| Twitter | 42 | 10.50 |
| Other | 22 | 5.50 |
| Total | 400 | 100 |

### 4.3.3 Information on digital marketing opinions of culture in Australia shows mean and standard deviation.

Table 4.3.3: To show mean and standard deviation from the digital marketing opinions of culture in Australia on Website.

| The digital marketing (Website) | $\bar{X}$ | S.D. | Meaning |
|---|---|---|---|
| 1. You often visit the store's main website to buy products. | 3.90 | 0.30 | High |
| 2. You often buy products on websites that are easy to use, and do not complex. | 3.97 | 0.18 | High |
| 3. You often buy products on websites that are reliable. | 3.99 | 0.99 | High |
| 4. You often click the banner ad to access the homepage of the website, and choose to buy products. | 3.08 | 0.27 | Moderate |
| Total | 3.73 | 0.43 | High |

Table 4.3.4: To show mean and standard deviation from the digital marketing opinions of culture in Australia on Content Marketing.

| The digital marketing (Content Marketing) | $\bar{X}$ | S.D. | Meaning |
|---|---|---|---|
| 1. You are always interested in content that provides useful information about product. | 3.05 | 0.20 | Moderate |
| 2. You are often interested in communicating with images or storytelling with pictures. | 3.17 | 0.37 | Moderate |
| 3. You are always interested in graphics that are short, concise and easy to understand. | 3.07 | 0.25 | Moderate |
| 4. You are always interested in content that has both content and entertainment. | 3.18 | 0.38 | Moderate |

## Table 4.3.5: To show mean and standard deviation from the digital marketing opinions of culture in Australia on E-Mail Marketing.

| The digital marketing (E-Mail Marketing) | $\overline{X}$ | S.D. | Meaning |
|---|---|---|---|
| 1. You receive an email with news or promotions and are interested. | 3.81 | 0.39 | High |
| 2. You get benefits through email and are impressed. | 3.87 | 0.34 | High |
| 3. You receive information about the product and purchase via email. | 3.80 | 0.40 | High |
| The digital marketing (E-Mail Marketing) | $\overline{X}$ | S.D. | Meaning |
| 4. You can communicate quickly and interact with the store easily. | 3.90 | 0.40 | High |
| Total | 3.84 | 0.36 | High |

## Table 4.3.6: To show mean and standard deviation from the digital marketing opinions of culture in Australia on Search Engine Optimization.

| The digital marketing (Search Engine Optimization) | $\overline{X}$ | S.D. | Meaning |
|---|---|---|---|
| 1. When searching for a store, you usually click to enter the store's first address. | 3.93 | 0.25 | High |
| 2. When you find the shop on the first page, you felt the shop that is credible. | 3.90 | 0.30 | High |
| 3. You often choose to click a website with short web names / easy to understand and enter only important word. | 3.92 | 0.27 | High |
| 4. You often choose to click on websites that have advertisements on websites (Search Engine like Google). | 3.87 | 0.33 | High |
| Total | 3.90 | 0.29 | High |

## Table 4.3.7: To show mean and standard deviation from the digital marketing opinions of culture in Australia on Social Media Marketing.

| The digital marketing (Social Media Marketing) | $\bar{X}$ | S.D. | Meaning |
|---|---|---|---|
| 1. You often click to follow various social fan pages to receive information of store. | 3.95 | 0.22 | High |
| 2. You feel that social media is a way to update convenient and fast information. | 3.90 | 0.31 | High |
| 3. You are interested in seeing advertisements or product promotions through various social media. | 3.92 | 0.27 | High |
| 4. You often use social media to find information and buy product. | 3.87 | 0.33 | High |
| Total | 3.91 | 0.28 | High |

### 4.3.7 Information on digital marketing opinions about buying decisions of culture in Australia shows mean and standard deviation.

## Table 4.3.8: To show mean and standard deviation from the digital marketing opinions about buying decisions of culture in Australia.

| Buying Decisions of Culture in Australia | $\bar{X}$ | S.D. | Meaning |
|---|---|---|---|
| 1. You search for information or reviews of products in your culture from the Internet to help in making a purchase decision. | 3.89 | 0.30 | High |
| 2. You are satisfied with the purchase of products through the digital marketing which will be introduced by others in your culture and want to come back to buy again. | 3.87 | 0.33 | High |
| 3. Each culture in Australia is different, and the ability to react to an online advertisement is affected in purchasing. | 3.89 | 0.30 | High |
| 4. You choose to buy products through the digital marketing because you meet the needs and convenience for your culture. | 3.78 | 0.41 | High |

## 4.3.7 Information on digital marketing opinions about buying decisions of culture in Australia shows mean and standard deviation.

Table 4.3.9: To show mean and standard deviation from the digital marketing opinions about buying decisions of culture in Australia.

| Buying Decisions of Culture in Australia | $\overline{X}$ | S.D. | Meaning |
|---|---|---|---|
| 5.You compare product information in qualification, reliable, price and promotion to choose the best option for your culture. | 3.84 | 0.36 | High |
| Total | 3.85 | 0.15 | High |

## 4.4 INFERENTIAL STATISTICS

Table 4.4.1: To show the digital marketing strategy development affected the cultures in Australia by using simple regression statistics.

### Coefficients[a]

| Model | Unstandardized Coefficients | | Standardized Coefficients | t | Sig. |
|---|---|---|---|---|---|
| | B | Std. Error | Beta | | |
| 1  (Constant) | 2.267 | .165 | | 13.745 | .000 |
| Buying Decisions of Culture in Australia | .423 | .043 | .446 | 9.936 | .000 |

a. Dependent Variable: You often visit the store's main website to buy products.

## Coefficients[a]

| Model | Unstandardized Coefficients | | Standardized Coefficients | t | Sig. |
|---|---|---|---|---|---|
| | B | Std. Error | Beta | | |
| 1   (Constant) | 2.890 | .094 | | 30.595 | .000 |
| Buying Decisions of Culture in Australia | .279 | .024 | .498 | 11.442 | .000 |

a. Dependent Variable: You often buy products on websites that are easy to use, and do not complex.

## Coefficients[a]

| Model | Unstandardized Coefficients | | Standardized Coefficients | t | Sig. |
|---|---|---|---|---|---|
| | B | Std. Error | Beta | | |
| 1   (Constant) | 3.659 | .059 | | 62.233 | .000 |
| Buying Decisions of Culture in Australia | .086 | .015 | .273 | 5.657 | .000 |

a. Dependent Variable: You often buy products on websites that are reliable.

## Coefficients[a]

| Model | Unstandardized Coefficients | | Standardized Coefficients | t | Sig. |
|---|---|---|---|---|---|
| | B | Std. Error | Beta | | |
| 1   (Constant) | 3.659 | .059 | | 62.233 | .000 |
| Buying Decisions of Culture in Australia | .086 | .015 | .273 | 5.657 | .000 |

a. Dependent Variable: You often buy products on websites that are reliable.

## Coefficients<sup>a</sup>

| Model | Unstandardized Coefficients | | Standardized Coefficients | | |
|---|---|---|---|---|---|
| | B | Std. Error | Beta | t | Sig. |
| 1    (Constant) | 2.747 | .163 | | 16.816 | .000 |
| Buying Decisions of Culture in Australia | .086 | .042 | .101 | 2.028 | .043 |

a. Dependent Variable: You often click the banner ad to access the homepage of the website, and choose to buy products.

## Coefficients<sup>a</sup>

| Model | Unstandardized Coefficients | | Standardized Coefficients | | |
|---|---|---|---|---|---|
| | B | Std. Error | Beta | t | Sig. |
| 1    (Constant) | 7.323 | .083 | | 88.468 | .000 |
| Buying Decisions of Culture in Australia | -1.079 | .021 | -.930 | -50.461 | .000 |

a. Dependent Variable: You are always interested in content that provides useful information about product.

## Coefficients<sup>a</sup>

| Model | Unstandardized Coefficients | | Standardized Coefficients | | |
|---|---|---|---|---|---|
| | B | Std. Error | Beta | t | Sig. |
| 1    (Constant) | 5.305 | .105 | | 50.402 | .000 |
| Buying Decisions of Culture in Australia | -.580 | .027 | -.730 | -21.328 | .000 |

a. Dependent Variable: You are always interested in graphics that are short, concise and easy to understand.

## Coefficients[a]

| Model | Unstandardized Coefficients | | Standardized Coefficients | | |
| --- | --- | --- | --- | --- | --- |
| | B | Std. Error | Beta | t | Sig. |
| 1    (Constant) | 7.380 | .102 | | 72.356 | .000 |
| Buying Decisions of Culture in Australia | -1.089 | .026 | -.901 | -41.339 | .000 |

a. Dependent Variable: You are always interested in content that has both content and entertainment

## Coefficients[a]

| Model | Unstandardized Coefficients | | Standardized Coefficients | | |
| --- | --- | --- | --- | --- | --- |
| | B | Std. Error | Beta | t | Sig. |
| 1    (Constant) | -.396 | .107 | | -3.710 | .000 |
| Buying Decisions of Culture in Australia | 1.092 | .028 | .893 | 39.640 | .000 |

a. Dependent Variable: You receive an email with news or promotions and are interested.

## Coefficients[a]

| Model | Unstandardized Coefficients | | Standardized Coefficients | | |
| --- | --- | --- | --- | --- | --- |
| | B | Std. Error | Beta | t | Sig. |
| 1    (Constant) | -.115 | .069 | | -1.681 | .094 |
| Buying Decisions of Culture in Australia | 1.031 | .018 | .946 | 58.178 | .000 |

a. Dependent Variable: You get benefits through email and are impressed.

## Coefficients[a]

| Model | Unstandardized Coefficients | | Standardized Coefficients | t | Sig. |
|---|---|---|---|---|---|
| | B | Std. Error | Beta | | |
| 1 (Constant) | -.460 | .123 | | -3.749 | .000 |
| Buying Decisions of Culture in Australia | 1.104 | .032 | .868 | 34.811 | .000 |

a. Dependent Variable: You receive information about the product and purchase via email.

## Coefficients[a]

| Model | Unstandardized Coefficients | | Standardized Coefficients | t | Sig. |
|---|---|---|---|---|---|
| | B | Std. Error | Beta | | |
| 1 (Constant) | .415 | .069 | | 5.981 | .000 |
| Buying Decisions of Culture in Australia | .902 | .018 | .930 | 50.377 | .000 |

a. Dependent Variable: You can communicate quickly and interact with the store easily.

## Coefficients[a]

| Model | Unstandardized Coefficients | | Standardized Coefficients | t | Sig. |
|---|---|---|---|---|---|
| | B | Std. Error | Beta | | |
| 1 (Constant) | 1.695 | .105 | | 16.105 | .000 |
| Buying Decisions of Culture in Australia | .580 | .027 | .730 | 21.328 | .000 |

a. Dependent Variable: When searching for a store, you usually click to enter the store's first address

## Coefficients[a]

| Model | Unstandardized Coefficients | | Standardized Coefficients | | |
| | B | Std. Error | Beta | t | Sig. |
|---|---|---|---|---|---|
| 1  (Constant) | .500 | .074 | | 6.742 | .000 |
| Buying Decisions of Culture in Australia | .881 | .019 | .917 | 45.968 | .000 |

a. Dependent Variable: When you find the shop on the first page, you felt the shop that is credible.

## Coefficients[a]

| Model | Unstandardized Coefficients | | Standardized Coefficients | | |
| | B | Std. Error | Beta | t | Sig. |
|---|---|---|---|---|---|
| 1  (Constant) | 1.268 | .100 | | 12.700 | .000 |
| Buying Decisions of Culture in Australia | .687 | .026 | .800 | 26.641 | .000 |

a. Dependent Variable: You often choose to click a website with short web names / easy to understand and enter only important word.

## Coefficients[a]

| Model | Unstandardized Coefficients | | Standardized Coefficients | | |
| | B | Std. Error | Beta | t | Sig. |
|---|---|---|---|---|---|
| 1  (Constant) | -.033 | .064 | | -.516 | .606 |
| Buying Decisions of Culture in Australia | 1.012 | .017 | .950 | 60.996 | .000 |

a. Dependent Variable: You often choose to click on websites that have advertisements on websites (Search Engine like Google).

## Coefficients[a]

| Model | Unstandardized Coefficients | | Standardized Coefficients | t | Sig. |
|---|---|---|---|---|---|
| | B | Std. Error | Beta | | |
| 1 (Constant) | 2.293 | .105 | | 21.892 | .000 |
| Buying Decisions of Culture in Australia | .430 | .027 | .623 | 15.878 | .000 |

a. Dependent Variable: You often click to follow various social fan pages to receive information of store.

## Coefficients[a]

| Model | Unstandardized Coefficients | | Standardized Coefficients | t | Sig. |
|---|---|---|---|---|---|
| | B | Std. Error | Beta | | |
| 1 (Constant) | .415 | .069 | | 5.981 | .000 |
| Buying Decisions of Culture in Australia | .902 | .018 | .930 | 50.377 | .000 |

a. Dependent Variable: You feel that social media is a way to update convenient and fast information.

## Coefficients[a]

| Model | Unstandardized Coefficients | | Standardized Coefficients | t | Sig. |
|---|---|---|---|---|---|
| | B | Std. Error | Beta | | |
| 1 (Constant) | 1.354 | .101 | | 13.355 | .000 |
| Buying Decisions of Culture in Australia | .666 | .026 | .787 | 25.429 | .000 |

a. Dependent Variable: You are interested in seeing advertisements or product promotions through various social media.

## Coefficients[a]

| Model | Unstandardized Coefficients | | Standardized Coefficients | | |
|---|---|---|---|---|---|
| | B | Std. Error | Beta | t | Sig. |
| 1   (Constant) | .088 | .065 | | 1.350 | .178 |
| Buying Decisions of Culture in Australia | .982 | .017 | .947 | 58.586 | .000 |

a. Dependent Variable: You often use social media to find information and buy product.

## 4.5 CONCLUSION

From the study of developing an appropriate digital marketing strategy model for culture in Australia, the researcher concluded a diagram to highlight the importance of developing an appropriate digital marketing strategy model for culture in Australia as follows:

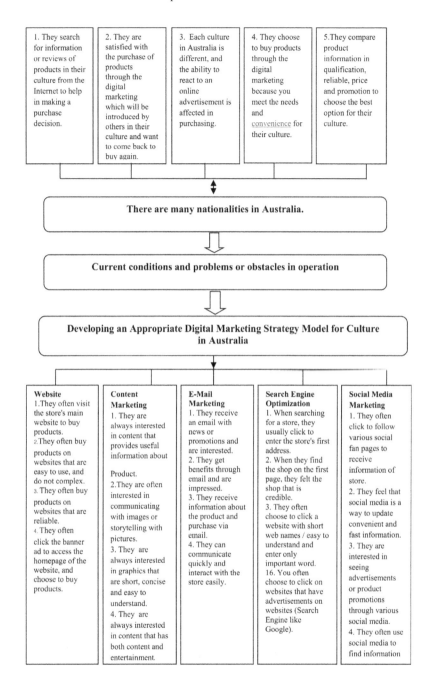

| 1. They search for information or reviews of products in their culture from the Internet to help in making a purchase decision. | 2. They are satisfied with the purchase of products through the digital marketing which will be introduced by others in their culture and want to come back to buy again. | 3. Each culture in Australia is different, and the ability to react to an online advertisement is affected in purchasing. | 4. They choose to buy products through the digital marketing because you meet the needs and convenience for their culture. | 5.They compare product information in qualification, reliable, price and promotion to choose the best option for their culture. |

**There are many nationalities in Australia.**

**Current conditions and problems or obstacles in operation**

**Developing an Appropriate Digital Marketing Strategy Model for Culture in Australia**

| **Website** | **Content Marketing** | **E-Mail Marketing** | **Search Engine Optimization** | **Social Media Marketing** |
|---|---|---|---|---|
| 1.They often visit the store's main website to buy products. 2.They often buy products on websites that are easy to use, and do not complex. 3. They often buy products on websites that are reliable. 4. They often click the banner ad to access the homepage of the website, and choose to buy products. | 1. They are always interested in content that provides useful information about Product. 2.They are often interested in communicating with images or storytelling with pictures. 3. They are always interested in graphics that are short, concise and easy to understand. 4. They are always interested in content that has both content and entertainment. | 1. They receive an email with news or promotions and are interested. 2. They get benefits through email and are impressed. 3. They receive information about the product and purchase via email. 4. They can communicate quickly and interact with the store easily. | 1. When searching for a store, they usually click to enter the store's first address. 2. When they find the shop on the first page, they felt the shop that is credible. 3. They often choose to click a website with short web names / easy to understand and enter only important word. 16. You often choose to click on websites that have advertisements on websites (Search Engine like Google). | 1. They often click to follow various social fan pages to receive information of store. 2. They feel that social media is a way to update convenient and fast information. 3. They are interested in seeing advertisements or product promotions through various social media. 4. They often use social media to find information |

# Jarungjit Tiautrakul's Marketing Strategy Model for Culture in Australia

## 4.6 ANALYSIS

This chapter will interpretation of results as follows:

### 1. General information of the respondents

In fact, general information of the respondents responded to the questionnaire using descriptive statistics found that the sample group that responded to the questionnaire was mostly female with 302 persons or 75.50 percent , and male: 98 persons or 24.50 percent.

In terms of age, it was found that the majority of sample respondents aged 21-30 years from 205 persons: 51.20 percent, followed by those under the age of 20 or equivalent, totaling 99 persons: 24.80 percent. Age 31-40 years, 62 persons: 15.50 percent, aged 41-50 years, 23 people: 5.80 percent, and the minimum age was 51 years and above, number 11: 2.80 percent.

In terms of status, it was found that the sample who responded to the questionnaires mostly had single status of 350 persons: 87.50 percent, followed by marital status, 44 persons,: 11.00 percent, and the least divorced / widowed status of 6 people: 1.50 each

In terms of level of education, it was found that the majority of respondents had 236 undergraduates: 59.00 percent, followed by high school students, 72 persons: 18.00 percent, master's degree 43 students: 10.80, lower than high school students, 30 people: 7.50 percent, diploma or equivalent, 18 people: 4.50 percent and the smallest Ph.D., 1 person: 0.30 percent

In terms of occupation, it was found that the respondents with the most questionnaires had a student of 156 persons: 39.00 percent, followed by a career of private company employees of 142 persons, accounting for 35.50 percent, owned by private company employees of 54 people: 13.50 percent, state enterprise employees / government officials, 25 persons,: 6.30 percent, other occupations, 14 persons: 3.50 percent, and the smallest, 9 housewives / butlers: 2.30 percent.

In terms of average monthly income, it was found that the majority of respondents had an average monthly income. 444-888 dollar, 151 persons: 37.80 percent, followed by lower than or equal to 444 dollar,

141 persons: 35.30 percent, with income 888-1332 dollar, 68 people: 17.00 percent, with income 2,219 or over dollar 16 people: 4.00 percent, with income of 1,332-1,776 dollar, with 13 persons: 3.30 percent and the least earning 1,776-2,220 dollar, 11 persons: 2.80 percent.

In terms of hobby, it was found that the sample group that responded to the questionnaires mostly 182 surfing the Internet users: 45.50 percent, followed by watching movies / listening to music, 98 people: 24.50 percent, playing sports / games, 41 people: 10.30 percent, shopping for 26 people: 6.50 percent, reading 25 people: 6.30 percent, pets of 15 people: 3.80 percent, and the other hobbies 13 people: 3.30 percent.

In terms of nationality, it was found that the sample group that responded to the questionnaires mostly 182 Chinese: 45.50 percent, followed by Philippians, 98 people: 24.50 percent, Aboriginals, 41 people: 10.30 percent, Indians, 26 people: 6.50 percent, Britons, 25 people: 6.30 percent, African of 15 people: 3.80 percent, and the other nationality 13 people: 3.30 percent.

### 2. Information on the behavior of buying products and services through the electronic commerce business.

The sample group that responded to the questionnaire on the behavior of buying products and services through the electronic commerce business were described as follows:

The reason for choosing to buy products and services through e-commerce, most respondents (163 people: 40.80 percent) bought because there were interesting promotional items, followed by cheaper than the general market (123 people: 30.80 percent), confident in safety systems (51 people: 12.80 percent), others (37 people: 9.30 percent), and others persuaded (26 people: 6.50 percent) respectively.

People who influence the decision to purchase products or services through e-commerce, most respondents decided by themselves (278 people: 69.50 percent), followed by notices from those who used that product or service before (57 people: 14.20 percent), friends /

colleagues (28 people: 7.00 percent), family members (27 people: 6.80 percent), and famous people (10 people: 2.50 percent)

On the frequency of buying products or services through e-commerce per month, most respondents buy 1-2 times (182 people: 45.50 percent), followed by less than 1 times (145 people: 36.30 percent), buying 5-6 times (47 people: 11.80 percent), 7 times or more (10 people: 2.50 percent).

The price of products or services that are purchased via e-commerce per time, most respondents bought 23 - 45 dollar (172 people, : 43.00 percent), followed by not more than 22 dollar (130 people: 32.50 percent), 46 – 67 dollar (59 people: 14.80 percent), and 68 or more 68 dollar (39 people: 9.80 percent).

The reason for choosing to buy products or services through ecommerce, most respondents want convenience because they can choose to purchase 24 hours a day (199 people: 49.80 percent), followed by available in a variety of normal rather than buying in general market (72 people:18.00 percent), cheaper than general market buying is the same with the ability to study opinions from those who have used the service before (61 people: 15.30 percent), and the other 7people: 1.80 per cent).

The most frequently used equipment to access the electronic commerce business. Most respondents used smartphones (349 people: 87.30 percent), followed by Notebook / PC (37 people: 9.30 percent), and tablet (14 people: 3.50 percent).

The time period when using the internet to buy products or services, most respondents chose to buy at 16.01-20.00 hrs, equal to 20.01-24.00 hrs. (154 people: 38.50 percent), followed by 12.01-16.00 hrs. (63 people: 15.80 percent), at 08.01-12.00. (23 people: 5.80 percent), at 00.01-04.00 hrs. (5 people: 1.30 percent), and 04.01-08.00 hrs. (1 person: 0.30 percent).

Types of products or services that are most frequently purchased via electronic commerce, most respondents chose 182 fashion items (182 people: 45.50 percent), followed by health and beauty products (98 people: 24.50 percent), IT equipment (46 people: 11.50 percent), others (31 people: 7.80 percent), household (24 people: 6.00 percent), and travel / tourism (19 people: 4.80 percent).

Channels of e-commerce businesses used to purchase products or services, most respondents chose Facebook channel (123 people: 30.80 percent), followed by Website (110 people: 27.50 percent), Instagram (84 people: 21.00 percent), Twitter (42 people: 10.50 percent), others (22 people: 5.50 percent), and Line (19 people: 4.80 percent).

### 3. Information on digital marketing opinions of culture in Australia on website.

The result was found that the overall respondents' opinions were at Mean score of 3.73 and Standard deviation at 0.43. The variable that got the highest score was opinion toward buying products on websites that are reliable. (Mean = 3.99, SD = 0.99), followed by buying products on websites that are easy to use, and do not complex. (Mean = 3.97, SD = 0.18), visit the store's main website to buy products. (Mean = 3.08, SD = 0.27), and clicking the banner ad to access the homepage of the website, and choose to buy products. (Mean = 3.08, SD = 0.27) respectively.

### 4. The digital marketing opinions of culture in Australia on Content Marketing.

The result was found that the overall respondents' opinions were at Mean score of 3.12 and Standard deviation at 0.30. The variable that got the highest score was opinion toward "you are always interested in content that has both content and entertainment." (Mean = 3.18, SD = 0.38), followed by "you are often interested in communicating with images or storytelling with pictures." (Mean = 3.17, SD = 0.25), "you are always interested in graphics that are short, concise and easy to understand." (Mean = 3.07, SD = 0.25), and "you are always interested in content that provides useful information about product." (Mean = 3.05, SD = 0.20) respectively.

## 5. The digital marketing opinions of culture in Australia on E-Mail Marketing.

The result was found that the overall respondents' opinions were at Mean score of 3.84 and Standard deviation at 0.36. The variable that got the highest score was opinion toward "you can communicate quickly and interact with the store easily." (Mean = 3.90, SD = 0.30), followed by "you get benefits through email and are impressed." (Mean = 3.87, SD = 0.34), "you receive an email with news or promotions and are interested." (Mean = 3.81, SD = 0.39), and "you receive information about the product and purchase via email." (Mean = 3.80, SD = 0.40) respectively.

## 6. The digital marketing opinions of culture in Australia on Search Engine Optimization.

The result was found that the overall respondents' opinions were at Mean score of 3.90 and Standard deviation at 0.29. The variable that got the highest score was opinion toward " when searching for a store, you usually click to enter the store's first address." (Mean = 3.93, SD = 0.25), followed by "you often choose to click a website with short web names / easy to understand and enter only important word." (Mean = 3.92, SD = 0.27), " when you find the shop on the first page, you felt the shop that is credible." (Mean = 3.90, SD = 0.30), and "you often choose to click on websites that have advertisements on websites (Search Engine like Google)." (Mean = 3.87, SD = 0.33) respectively.

## 7. The digital marketing opinions of culture in Australia on Social Media Marketing.

The result was found that the overall respondents' opinions were at Mean score of 3.74 and Standard deviation at 0.79. The variable that got the highest score was opinion toward "you feel that social media is a way to update convenient and fast information." (Mean = 3.91, SD = 0.93), followed by "you often use social media to find information and buy product." (Mean = .83, SD = 0.96), " often click to follow various social fan pages to receive information of store." (Mean = 3.65, SD

= 1.03), and "you are interested in seeing advertisements or product promotions through various social media." (Mean = 3.55, SD = 0.95) respectively.

## 8. The digital marketing opinions about buying decisions of culture in Australia.

The result was found that the overall respondents' opinions were at Mean score of 3.76 and Standard deviation at 0.93. The variable that got the highest score were opinion toward "you search for information or reviews of products in your culture from the Internet to help in making a purchase decision.", and "each culture in Australia is different, and the ability to react to an online advertisement is affected in purchasing." (Mean = 3.94, SD = 0.90), followed by "you are satisfied with the purchase of products through the digital marketing which will be introduced by others in your culture and want to come back to buy again." (Mean = 3.85, SD = 0.96), " you compare product information in qualification, reliable, price and promotion to choose the best option for your culture.." (Mean = 3.83, SD = 0.96), and "you choose to buy products through the digital marketing because you meet the needs and convenience for your culture." (Mean = 3.26, SD = 0.96) respectively.

### Questions about alternatives

Applications of modern digital marketing techniques are what most marketers do to win more customers and make their products known. The type of messages used in marketing aims at involving and engaging the potential customer at its best. Engagement is only made possible when the message used reflects what the target audience like. This means that understanding the behaviour and personal values of the target audience are an ingredient of marketing success. In Australia, there are diverse cultures from all over the world (Clancy, 2004, p. 7). The kind of message used in digital marketing platform should please and engage all cultures. Due to diverse cultural preferences, digital marketers often offend other culture while engaging the other positively (Guang and Trotte, 2012, p. 6461-6466). Most of the marketers, if they intend to market a product to whole Australians, decide to please the majority and displease the minority.

The decision to offend the minority is not a positive outcome of firms who intend to increases sales and provision of services. Most firms, who seek to target the entire Australian audience, often, have a problem in tailoring content to suit diverse background. Effective marketing is the one that the audience understands and connect with the marketer. Effective connection with the audience often results in owning and connecting with the brand. Targeting a multicultural society means having a cross-cultural marketing strategy (Retnowati, 2015, p. 341).

Digital marketers need to have a better understanding of the marketing content, bearing in mind the effect of the marketing strategy in a diverse culture. They should be able to understand the behavior and the needs of each culture, the language and their way of life. Most firms that connect with the multicultural diversity aligns themselves with a wide audience, and probably business success (Yalcin and Cimendag, 2012, p. 23). The reverse is true, mainly if the firm targets the entire population of Australia, with diverse cultural backgrounds. The presence of diverse culture and behavior of the Australian audience calls for a different approach to modern digital marketing. There is limited research on the way firms design their digital marketing techniques in respect to heterogeneous culture. Although several studies have been done on the effects of digital marketing techniques on consumers (Hendrix, 2014, p. 250; Merisavo, 2006, p. 28-30), there is limited understanding of the way culture influence digital marketing techniques in Australia. It is also not clear whether firms have reacted positively to the diverse cultural audience in Australia or have retained their traditional marketing strategies in digital marketing. Since modern digital marketing techniques seek to connect with the audience in a higher level, by involving the audience in the development of the brand and marketing, there should be a significant success resulting from improved and personalized marketing approach undertaken. This research also seeks to find developing an appropriate digital marketing strategy model for culture in Australia. This research seeks to answer the following questions:

1) What are opinions of the digital marketing strategy model that is suitable for culture in Australia?

2) Does the digital marketing strategy development affected the cultures in Australia?

# CHAPTER 5
# General Discussions

**Discussion of the findings**
**1. Discussion of finding one**

In this section, the results of the study were discussed as follows:

The opinions of the digital marketing strategy model that is suitable for culture in Australia were found that there were 5 digital marketing strategy models: websites, content marketing, email, search engine optimization and social media. Website was the suitable for cultural in Australia. The variable that got the highest score was opinion toward buying products on websites that are reliable. (Mean = 3.99, SD = 0.99), followed by buying products on websites that are easy to use, and do not complex. (Mean = 3.97, SD = 0.18), visit the store's main website to buy products. (Mean = 3.08, SD = 0.27), and clicking the banner ad to access the homepage of the website, and choose to buy products. (Mean = 3.08, SD = 0.27) respectively. It might be that it consistent with the concept of the Pattharawadee Rienmanee (2012). She found that the website is one of the internet marketing media that has played a role in almost all types of business, whether in the form of a company, shop or general business in every parallel of the business because the website can respond and cover consumers or target groups that have no limit because the target group can visit the website information via the internet all over the world 24 hours a day.

Therefore, it can be concluded that the website is a storefront that has no scheduled opening and closing and no holidays. Therefore, having a website is very necessary if you want products and services to connect with consumers on the online world. Moreover, these results were consistent with the concept of Piyavit Jenakijjaepaiboon (2010) who stated that the website is called as the location of people who have their own web pages on the Internet which is obtained from registering with the space rental service provider on the Internet system. When registering in the desired name, you can create a webpage and send it to the service center to be put on the Internet which is considered to have their own website, and the website is the source of the web collection in many pages on the same subject are included, but one thing in offering stories on websites that are different from television programs, magazine content, or newspaper because the work on the web will never end. This is because we can change and add information on the website in any time, and each webpage will be linked within the website or to other websites, so readers can read it in a short time.

Content marketing was the suitable for cultural in Australia. The variable that got the highest score was opinion toward "you are always interested in content that has both content and entertainment." (Mean = 3.18, SD = 0.38), followed by "you are often interested in communicating with images or storytelling with pictures." (Mean = 3.17, SD = 0.25), "you are always interested in graphics that are short, concise and easy to understand." (Mean = 3.07, SD = 0.25), and "you are always interested in content that provides useful information about product." (Mean = 3.05, SD = 0.20) respectively. It might be because it consistent with the concept of the Taylor (2013) who stated that 90 percent of consumers prefer content marketing because it is more useful than other forms of presentation.

In addition, these results were consistent with the research of Gupta (2004) who found that the importance of content marketing is growing that is explained from statistics and the fact that 60% of the B2B business model that entrepreneurs say brands with content marketing helps consumers to make better buying decisions, while 61% of consumers tend to buy products from companies that offer custom content.

E-mail marketing was the suitable for cultural in Australia. The variable that got the highest score was opinion toward "you can communicate quickly and interact with the store easily." (Mean = 3.90, SD = 0.30), followed by "you get benefits through email and are impressed." (Mean = 3.87, SD = 0.34), "you receive an email with news or promotions and are interested." (Mean = 3.81, SD = 0.39), and "you receive information about the product and purchase via email." (Mean = 3.80, SD = 0.40) respectively. It might be that it consistent with the concept of the Jackson and De Cormier (2010) who stated that email is recognized as a communication with marketers to create a relationship that is allowed and real-time interaction with customers. Moreover, these results were consistent with the concept of Kantasit Lertpraingam (2010) who stated that the advantages of electronic mail marketing include direct communication with customers and target groups. Moreover, it's fast and able to respond immediately with low cost, and can communicate with many people at a time. Although the use of electronic mail marketing has advantages, it must also be careful in the delivery of electronic mail in large quantities or without content (Spam). Before using marketing through electronic mails, it must first be accepted by the customers or target group of account owners, and also be able to stop receiving news because it may affect the image of the brand at an irreparable level.

Search engine optimization was the suitable for cultural in Australia. The variable that got the highest score was opinion toward " when searching for a store, you usually click to enter the store's first address." (Mean = 3.93, SD = 0.25), followed by "you often choose to click a website with short web names / easy to understand and enter only important word." (Mean = 3.92, SD = 0.27), " when you find the shop on the first page, you felt the shop that is credible." (Mean = 3.90, SD = 0.30), and "you often choose to click on websites that have advertisements on websites (Search Engine like Google)." (Mean = 3.87, SD = 0.33) respectively. It might be that it consistent with the concept of Sezgin (2009) who stated that search engine optimization (SEO) makes the website which appears on the top-rank to display search results for some certain keywords. There are many factors that make the website move up to the top. The most effective way to attract the attention of many users is to connect with search engine optimization because search engine optimization is based on keywords that are appropriate to the website, and can use search with search engines. In order to optimize a website according to search engines, it must be appropriate to the technical conditions. In addition, these results were consistent with Rutz and Bucklin (2011) who found that consumers still choose to receive product information from online, search engine optimization (SEO) becomes increasingly important for integrated marketing communications. SEO planning usually begins with keyword analysis, which appropriate keywords are used and evaluated website content which is created to collect keywords, tags and other text.

Social media marketing was the suitable for cultural in Australia. The variable that got the highest score was opinion toward "you often click to follow various social fan pages to receive information of store." (Mean = 3.95, SD = 0.22), followed by "you are interested in seeing advertisements or product promotions through various social media." (Mean = 3.92, SD = 0.27), "you feel that social media is a way to update convenient and fast information." (Mean = 3.90, SD = 0.31), and "you often click to follow various social fan pages to receive information of store." (Mean = 3.87, SD = 0.33) respectively. It might be that it consistent with the concept of Weinberg and Pehlivan, (2011) who found that social media marketing enables customers to update information about new products and services at all times. It also helps customers to collect market data with relatively low costs (Gallaugher and Ransbotham, 2010) and can identify new market trends which facilitates the development and market orientation (Becker, Greve and Albers, 2009). It also helps to add real-time news, feedback, comments, complaints and suggestions (Trainor, Andzulis, Rapp and Agnihotri, 2014 ). People are now more involved with social media in communicating with friends, family and others (Labus and Stone, 2010). Social media marketing is therefore the most effective strategy to maintain outstanding customer relationships (King and Burgess, 2008).

In conclusion, Because there are different nationality in Australia, so these explain the opinions of the digital marketing strategy model (websites, content marketing, email, search engine optimization and social media)that are suitable for culture in Australia.

## 2. Discussion of finding two

The finding found that the digital marketing strategy development affected the cultures in Australia. The results of the study were discussed as follows: it was found that the Sig. value is 0.00 which was lower than the significance level 0.05. Therefore, the hypothesis is accepted that the digital marketing strategy development influences the cultures in Australia. When considering the coefficients in the standard score format (Beta), it is found that the value meaning that digital marketing strategy development has a positive influence on the consumers in the cultures in Australia. 1 digital unit has a greater effect on consumers in the cultures in Australia, and analyzing individual independent variables. It might be that it consistent with the concept of Tenderich (2014) who stated that spreadable content can only be attained through deeper understanding of the target audience and their cultures. There is no way a marketer can compose a successful message if the culture of the target audience is unknown. An effective content marketing must link with the emotions of the target audience. Culture includes ideas, and emotions that define that activities and the behaviour of the consumer. Moreover, these results were consistent with Makgosa (2012) who stated that a person can learn about the behaviour and culture of a certain country by studying the advertisements only. This is because advertisements are conveying messages regarding the behaviour, norm, and interests of national culture. It is a reflection of the countries believe and likes. In many advertisements, it is very easy to speculate on the issue of gender whether it is masculine of feminist's country. The advertisement must reflect what people believe in, and it is through this way that the country prides itself. In addition, the results were consistent with the concept of Chan (2015) who stated that Categorizing Australian culture based on Hofstede's cultural dimensions is complex. This is because the inhabitants are a mixture of varying cultures, some showing high power distance while other showing lower power distance. It is difficult to generalize the Australian cultural dimensions as each culture have different cultural dimensions, and the ability to react to an online advertisement is affected. This means for effective advertisement and development of relationship marketing; each brand needs to approach the Australian market cautiously. Moreover, the research of Wipada Phittayawirut and Nak Gulis (2015) was consistent with this research. Their study showed that digital marketing influencing consumers' response in approaching marketing information. Consumers' perception had the significant correlation to overall consumers' responses while lifestyle in category of average period in using digital media to access the marketing information per day and consumers' behavior in category of average frequency in using digital media had the significant correlation to consumers' responses in category of attention and desire.

These explain the digital marketing strategy development affected the cultures in Australia.

# Recommendations of Further Studies

The current study explored developing an appropriate digital marketing strategy model for culture in Australia. It would be interesting to recommend the following for further studies.

1) Suggesting to study additional factors such as Online PR factors, Mobile and Apps Marketing factors, Online Video and Viral factors, and ROI factors etc. to use the information for the strategic planning of e-commerce business in the future.

2) Suggesting to study other business groups to compare that digital marketing has influence on other culture or businesses that adjust to increase online channels that originally had only part of offline by studying other digital marketing tools influencing businesses such as brand building, awareness building, relationship building and sales stimulation, etc.

# Bibliograghy

1) Aaker. (2016). Digital marketing strategies that Millennials find appealing, motivating, or just annoying. *Journal of Strategic Marketing, 19*(6), 489-499.

2) Abs.gov.au. (2018). *2016 Census: Multicultural.* [online] Viewed 29 Oct. 2018<http://www.abs.gov.au/ausstats/abs@.nsf/lookup/Media%20Release3>

3) Allen. (2015). *eMarketing: The essential guide to digital marketing. Quirk eMarketing.*

4) An, D. and Meenan, P. (2016). *Why Marketers Should Care About Mobile PageSpeed.* [online] Think with Google. Viewed 29 Oct. 2018:<https://www.thinkwithgoogle.com/marketing resources/experiencedesign/mobile-page-speed-load-time/>

5) Armstrong, G., Adam, S., Denize, S., & Kotler, P. (2014). *Principles of marketing.* Pearson Australia.

6) Arun. (2015). A research on the role of digital media in the marketing strategy of luxury in Thailand which aimed to study the role and importance of digital media in the marketing strategy of the high fashion brands of the domestic market. *Master thesis, M.B.A., Bangkok University*, Bangkok.

7) Bunga and Methawee. (2015). L'Officiel Thailand online marketing strategies. *Master thesis, M.B.A., National Institute of Development Administration*, Bangkok.

8)  Bumrung and Chawanrat. (2017). Strategies for using advertising media on Internet media, website type of business that affects the receiving of information from the target group. *Nakhon Si Thammarat Rajabhat University*. Nakhon Si Thammarat.

9)  Chan, A. (2015). Marketing to Chinese- Australians. *Academy of Marketing Science 2015*, pp.120-136

10) Charinee and Pranee. (2016). Service marketing mix factors affecting the use of online banking transactions, Government Savings Bank in Chiang Rai Province. The University of the Thai Chamber Commerce. *Master thesis, M.B.A., Burapha University*, Bangkok.

11) Chombhak and Narapon. (2017). Farmer's behavior in using social network for sale rice on Facebook website group type. a case study of group Facebook name " buy –sell rice for help farmers". *Master thesis, M.B.A., Silpakorn University.*, Bangkok.

12) Etikan, I., Musa, S. and Alkassim, R. (2016). Comparison of Convenience Sampling and Purposive Sampling. *American Journal of Theoretical and Applied Statistics*, 5(1), pp.1-4.

13) Faqih, K. and Jaradat, M. (2015). Assessing the moderating effect of gender differences and individualism-collectivism at individual-level on the adoption of mobile commerce technology: TAM3 perspective. *Journal of Retailing and Consumer Services*, 22, pp.37-52.

14) Guntalee. (2018). The identification of research problems in digital marketing for Thailand in the future. *Chulalongkorn Business school, Chulalongkorn University*. Bangkok.

15) Hendrix, P. (2014). How Digital Technologies Are Enabling Consumers and Transforming the Practice of Marketing. *Journal of Marketing Theory and Practice*, 22(2), pp.149-150.

16) Holliman, G., & Rowley, J. (2014). Business to business digital content marketing: marketers' perceptions of best practice. *Journal of research in interactive marketing*, 8(4), 269-293.

17) Jidapha. (2015). Social media marketing, trust and information system quality affecting products' purchase decision through Facebook Live of online customers in Bangkok. *Master thesis, M.B.A., Bangkok University*, Bangkok.

18) Karnpat. (2015). The development of marketing strategy and marketing communication under marketing 3.0 concept of Hi-Q Product Foods Company Limited. *Master thesis, M.B.A., Thammasat University*, Pathumthani.

19) Kedwadee. (2017). Analysis the tools of marketing communication affecting achievement Pong Hom Sri Jun brand of Thais teenagers in Bangkok. *Faculty of Management Science, Silpakorn University Phetchaburi IT Campus,* Petchburi

20) Kietzmann, J. H., Hermkens, K., McCarthy, I. P., & Silvestre, B. S. (2014). Social media? Get serious! Understanding the functional building blocks of social media. *Business horizons, 54*(3), 241-251.

21) Kwan. (2016). The possibility study of the strategic problems of the service infrastructure promotion from Thailand's digital economy policy. *Current Opinion in Psychology, 10*, 17-21.

22) Kotler, P., Kartajaya, H., & Setiawan, I. (2017). *Marketing 4.0: do tradicional ao digital.* Sextante.

23) Lamberton, C., & Stephen, A. T. (2016). A thematic exploration of digital, social media, and mobile marketing: Research evolution from 2000 to 2015 and an agenda for future inquiry. *Journal of Marketing, 80*(6), 146-172.

24) Leeflang, P. S., Verhoef, P. C., Dahlström, P., & Freundt, T. (2014). Challenges and solutions for marketing in a digital era. *European management journal, 32*(1), 1-12.

25) Maryam, S., Hormoz, M. and Ferido, A. (2014). Studying the relationship between brand and consumer loyalty in audio-video industry (Case study: Gonbad Kavoos city, Iran). *Advances in Applied Science Research*, 4(5), pp.278-281.

26) Montri, Sirawit, and Supot. (2017). *Digital marketing: global strategies from the world's leading experts.* John Wiley & Sons.

27) Montri, Sirawit, and Supot. (2017). Causal of digital marketing influencing hotel customers' satisfaction and loyalty in the Andaman Triangle Cluster, Thailand. *Journal of the Association of Researchers Vol.23 No.3.*

28) Nak and Wipada. (2015). digital marketing influencing consumers' response in approaching marketing information. *Journal of Consumer affairs, 43*(3), 389-418.

29) Nares. (2017). Digital marketing strategies that Millennials find appealing, motivating, or just annoying. *Journal of Strategic Marketing, 19*(6), 489-499.

30) Natthani. (2016). Digital marketing communications influencing on Lazada website online buying behavior in Bangkok. *Master thesis, M.B.A., Rajamangala University of Technology Thanyaburi,* Pathumthani.

31) 31.Natthaphon. (2015). Digital marketing: A framework, review and research agenda. *International Journal of Research in Marketing, 34*(1), 22-45.

32) Natthasak. (2014). The attitude of consumers towards businesses selling products and services online. *Journal of Digital Marketing, 19*(6), 488-500.

33) Oh, Y., Rezaei, S., Ismail, W. and Valaei, N. (2016). The effect of culture on attitude towards online advertising and online brands: applying Hofstede's cultural factors to Internet marketing. *International Journal of Internet Marketing and Advertising,* 10(4), pp.270-292.

34) Otero, T. and Rolán, X. (2016). Understanding Digital Marketing— Basics and Actions. *MBA,* pp.37-72.

35) Phattharawadee. (2015). Digital integrated marketing communication to affecting the service boxing in Bangkok. *Master thesis, M.B.A., Bangkok University,* Bangkok.

36) Pawut. (2014). Online business marketing strategy and usage behavior towards social; networks a case study of Facebook fanpage, Bangkok Metropolitan Area. *International Journal of Internet Marketing and Advertising*, 9(2), pp.260-282.

37) Pires G.D., Stanton J. (2015). The Marketing Relevance of Cultural Diversity: A Framework for Understanding Ethnicity and Acculturation. In *Proceedings of the 1998 Multicultural Marketing Conference* (pp. 279-292). Springer, Cham.

38) Pronpan. (2016). The influence of digital marketing toward consumer's buying decision via e-commerce in Bangkok. *Master thesis, M.B.A., Bangkok University*, Bangkok.

39) Priyanka, A. A. (2016). The role of digital branding on consumer retention: evaluating uses of social media in Bangladesh.

40) Rakkwan., 2017. Marketing communication of Mono music by Youtube channel. *Journal of Humanities ., Faculty of Humanities, Kasetsart University.* Bangkok.

41) Retnowati, Y., (2015). Challenges in Cross Cultural Advertising. *Humaniora*, 27(3), pp.341-346.

42) Rupin, C. (2015). Social media as a new engaging channel in brands' relationship marketing.

43) Somphob. (2017). Marketing strategy of online products. *Doctor of Business Administation. Pathumthani University*. Pathumthani.

44) Sheikhahmadi, A. (2014). Content marketing through data mining on Facebook social network. *Webology*, *11*(1), 1.

45) Tanakorn. (2017). Digital marketing communications toward taxi service applications in Bangkok, Thailand. *Journal of Business Administration. The Association of Private Higher Education Institutions of Thailand, 7(1).*

46) Taiminen, H. M., & Karjaluoto, H. (2015). The usage of digital marketing channels in SMEs. *Journal of Small Business and Enterprise Development*, *22*(4), 633-651.

47) Teimouri, H., Fanae, N., Jenab, K., Khoury, S. and Moslehpour, S. (2016). Studying the Relationship between Brand Personality and Customer Loyalty: A Case Study of Samsung Mobile Phone. *International Journal of Business and Management*, 11(2), pp.1-9.

48) Tiago, M. T. P. M. B., & Veríssimo, J. M. C. (2014). Digital marketing and social media: Why bother?. *Business horizons*, *57*(6), 703-708.

49) Wipada. (2017). Impact of social media used to create strategies for expanding opportunities and efficiency in small and medium enterprises. *IOSR Journal of Business and Management (IOSR-JBM)*.

50) Wymbs, C. (2014). Digital Marketing: The Time for a New "Academic Major" Has Arrived. *Journal of Marketing Education*, 33(1), pp.93-106.

51) Yasmin, A., Tasneem, S., & Fatema, K. (2015). Effectiveness of digital marketing in the challenging age: An empirical study. *International Journal of Management Science and Business Administration*, *1*(5), 69-80.